Living
at
the
Boundary

LAURA PERLS

Living at the Boundary

Edited by Joe Wysong

A
GESTALT JOURNAL
PUBLICATION

Contents

Introduction

Laura Perls preferred direct interchange to the written word. For over four decades she journeyed across North America and throughout Europe training mental health professionals and those in allied fields in the theory and practice of Gestalt therapy. Professionally active until a few months before her death at the age of eighty-five, she continued to travel widely and to conduct ongoing training and supervision groups at her apartment/office on Manhattan's Upper West Side.

Laura Posner Perls was a remarkable woman who touched the lives of all who knew her. Born in Germany, she was an inspiration to those she trained from the time she came to the United States in 1947 after having spent fifteen years as a practicing psychoanalyst in South Africa.

A biography of this extraordinary pioneer with roots in the tradition of classical Freudian psychoanalysis is in order, but these pages are not the place for it. We have decided instead to begin this collection with a transcription of an interview with Laura conducted by her friend and professional associate, Daniel Rosenblatt, Ph.D., and with a talk she gave at the 25th Anniversary Dinner of The New York Institute for Gestalt Therapy. Her conversation with Rosenblatt took place in the spring of 1984, shortly before her annual summer trip to Germany where she walked her beloved Alps. By far the most extensive interview Laura ever gave, it was originally recorded on videotape and has been edited for publication.

In the interview, Laura details her childhood experiences, her youth and education in Germany, and her professional activities in both South Africa and later in the United States. In her talk she specifically discusses the history of The New York Institute for Gestalt Therapy. We have identified the first two chapters as "History" and the remaining thirteen as "Theory."

Laura agreed to have us publish the English edition of *Living at the Boundary* shortly before she left for Europe for what became her final trip. She passed away shortly after her arrival in the town of her birth, Pforzheim, Germany. I was therefore unable to have Laura's assistance with the editing of the manuscript and am solely responsible for the changes made. *Living at the Boundary* had already been published in German by Edition Humanistische Psychologie and was translated and edited by Laura's close friend, Milan Sreckovic.

This is not, however, a retranslation of that edition. With the exception of "How to Educate Children for

Peace," which was written in German, the essays included were written in English and this edition was prepared from the original manuscripts. Also, I had access to materials unavailable to Sreckovic so this volume contains chapters that do not appear in the German edition.

I have refrained from making any editorial changes in chapters that were first published elsewhere and they appear as they did originally. I have included a publication history at the end of each chapter.

Joe Wysong
Highland, New York
Fall, 1991

Living
at
the
Boundary

Section I

HISTORY

1.

A Conversation with Laura Perls

DR: You are leaving for Europe in about a month. What will you be doing there?

LP: I will be doing three quantitative workshops in my home town, Pforzheim. A young Gestalt therapist just moved there and bought a house right around the corner from the friends that I always stay with when I'm visiting there. So it's very comfortable for me. I don't even have to use the car, I can just walk a few steps. It's about five minutes.

DR: How do you feel about being back in Pforzheim?

LP: I have gotten used to it again. I felt apprehensive the first couple of times I went back there after I hadn't been there since 1933 and once for a couple of days in 1957. But now I feel at home again, really. I still have some old friends there. In fact they are the only old friends I still have, friends of my generation who knew me when I was a child and who knew my parents and my family. And so it is like family.

DR: How different do you think Germany is today from what it was when you were there?

LP: Of course Frankfurt, when I was a student, was the most avant garde university in Germany, if not all of Europe. The faculty all lost their positions immediately when Hitler came to power and they immigrated, most of them, to New York and started the University in Exile which then amalgamated with the New School. There was Kurt Goldstein, Max Wertheimer, and Martin Buber.

DR: Well, those are all people who are important to Gestalt therapy.

LP: That's right.

DR: And its development.

LP: The University at Frankfurt is where I did all my psychological studies.

DR: Certainly one of the issues that people are very interested in is the antecedents of Gestalt therapy. And you just mentioned your own psychological background in Frankfurt.

LP: Well, I came comparatively late to psychology. I was first studying law and economics. I thought I would be getting into family law. It was very new at the time. I was one of the first women in Germany who went into law school. But then I got caught up by and really interested only in the psychological aspects of my studies. So, I switched. I actually have an aversion to it in a similar way in which I have an aversion to business activity which I was in first when I was a very little child. The business was downstairs and the apartment was upstairs and I went down every day when I was two or three years old and helped. A vocation. (laughs) Then my brother was born and I never did it again.

DR: So you hated your early business experience.

LP: Yes, didn't you?

DR: And pushed aside your legal experience. There is one early training you had that was important — music. And literature.

LP: Music was the most important. My mother played quite well. And I heard her playing from the cradle on. I started to play myself when I was five. I could read notes long before I could read anything else. I played four hands with her. By the time I was twelve or fourteen I played better than she did. I didn't know anything yet about anything else. But I got more interested, really, in philosophy, languages and psychology, and all kinds of other things.

DR: You're talking about music as an early training. How do you think it's influenced your work as a Gestalt therapist?

LP: Well, it linked up, actually, with the body work that I did from very early on. First when I was about eight. And later with a different school of eurythmics and modern dance which I maintained all through my life. I'm still doing some of the exercises and it keeps me going and I'm working with it a lot in my training groups because I think it's one of the essential supports.

DR: You never worked personally with Wilhelm Reich, but when Fritz did and he talked about the body armor do you remember making any connections then between what he was talking about and what you had as your own background and experience?

LP: Well, for me it linked up quite as a matter of course and it also linked up with Goldstein's concept of the organism as a totality.

DR: You mentioned the body as a support system. Do you want to say some more about that and how it linked up in the organism as a totality?

LP: Well, actually, what I am after is coordination and alignment so that most of the support in moving or in working comes from the undercarriage and from breathing so that the upper part of the body can be free for orientation and manipulation. And if one has to keep oneself upright from the shoulders and neck then you get kind of stuck here (gestures at neck area) and you are not really free.

DR: So what you're really demonstrating is the different points at which by not giving yourself proper support you can develop disturbances and interferences.

LP: That's right. Actually, all interference, all acquired interference, is part of the voluntary muscular system. This we know more in detail from Reich but I knew it already long before from my experience from dance.

DR: One of the things I recall is that, when you mention the voluntary muscular system developing interferences, you used to have a theory that the emotions had a particular muscular response, like disgust and anger being visceral. How much of that do you still hold, or have you modified it in any way?

LP: Well, of course, the primary automatic response is if you swallow something that is not digestible, you bring it up... and regurgitate. And that sets a pattern for swallowing anything else, as we say, mentally or intellectually or emotionally. Introjecting. Freud still thought that one learns through introjection. But that is a very limited learning, applied at the very early stage of human development. But then the pattern is set by the way you deal with solid food. Either chewing it, working it through...

DR: Well, that's always one of the revelations for me from Gestalt therapy that you and Fritz talked about is the necessity to destroy.

LP: I use the word destructure instead because destroying always implies some kind of hostility, while actually the destructuring and restructuring are the kinetic forces through which one grows.

DR: Well, I'm being more literal and staying close to the mastication process and although technically you're destructuring, what you're really doing is taking what's solid food and tearing it to bits with the teeth.

LP: This was developed in *Ego, Hunger and Aggression*.

DR: I remember being impressed with that concept of finding a way to take something and tear it apart or break it down, destructure it, to destroy and something good would come out of it. It wasn't just some kind of blind, hostile, angry act, but a necessary step to reach some other kind of an integration.

LP: It was something that started to interest me in Berlin when I had my first child. I got interested and did some research on the feeding and weaning of children.

DR: Well, that was one of the earliest departures from traditional psychoanalytic thinking.

LP: Fritz expanded my notes into a lecture he did for the 1936 International Psychoanalytic Congress at Marienbad which was then expanded into the section on mental metabolism in *Ego, Hunger and Aggression*.

DR: Then you also did some work on the dummy activity.

LP: I did the chapter on the dummy complex and the chapter on insomnia.

DR: If it was in 1936, and this is 1984, it's almost 50 years since the departure...

LP: Yes, then we called it a revision of Freudian analysis and we still called ourselves psychoanalysts. The expression "Gestalt therapy" came in with the next book, which was written with Paul Goodman.

DR: What made you change the term from revisionist psychoanalyst to Gestalt therapy?

LP: What we did I wanted to call "existential therapy" but at the time the term "existentialism" was understood mainly in the sense of Sartre and certain nihilistic attitudes so Fritz or Paul suggested "Gestalt therapy."

DR: Do you remember which one?

LP: I don't remember. At that time I kept myself on the margin of it. When we started the Institute I didn't want to be a member of the staff at all. I had never taught and I was so over-engaged in practice and travelling to Philadelphia once a week, and I still had the children in the house.

DR: When you mention starting the Institute, what was your input?

LP: Everything was talked through. It's very difficult to say now who put in what. I think Paul Goodman's influence was very important and I don't think that without him there would be a coherent theory of Gestalt therapy at all.

DR: When I first met you I was told that there were these left wing psychoanalysts, Fritz and Laura Perls.

LP: We actually worked in South Africa for thirteen years without any direct affiliation with any psychoanalytical group or any supervision so we could really do what we liked. We found out that the strict psychoanalytical approach was, in many cases, insufficient and didn't result in very much. We had people for ten and twelve years and they improved somewhat, but didn't really change essentially. I thought also that it became very boring. What the psychoanalytic technique does is avoid embarrassment and unease for the therapist as well as for the client. The client talks to the wall and the therapist sits behind the patient and they never face each other. There is no personal contact at all.

DR: It sounds like there isn't even good confluence there. Each one is off with his own.

LP: Of course not. There is a lot of separation and unclear boundaries which really leads to more introjection for the client.

DR: Well, with that discomfort with psychoanalytic office practice and with your own and Fritz's emerging theoretical points of view, can you indicate when you, or he, or you, he and Paul, felt you really wanted to begin again, or separate yourselves from psychoanalysis?

LP: It came very gradually in South Africa. When we came here the work on *Gestalt Therapy: Excitement and Growth in the Human Personality* started almost immediately, as soon as we met Paul Goodman. At that time Paul was in Reichian analysis. I had read his critical essays in South Africa, in a magazine edited by Dwight McDonald, *Politics*.

DR: So when the three of you came together, it was really with a strong background and interest in psycho-analysis.

LP: In Reichian analysis, which was already a deviation.

DR: And Reich was in New York at that time.

LP: Yes, but when Fritz visited him once in his set-up somewhere else in New York State, he was very grandiose and offended somehow that we didn't know anything about his Orgone work. In South Africa, of course, we didn't get any literature. There was hardly any mail coming from America, and certainly not anything about Reich's work in the United States. I'm not a scientist in that sense. Reich was much more of a scientist, really a biologist. Reich, I met, really, only once. I didn't know him personally at all. Fritz was with him for about two years, I think. Absolutely fascinated. And he would have gone on with him. But then when Hitler came into power, Reich got out before us.

DR: I remember Fritz saying, "I had four therapists and Wilhelm Reich was the best of them by far."

LP: Oh yes. I think he gained much. With a strictly Freudian approach, you couldn't get through. And I think that in my analysis with Carl Landauer, which in many ways was better than Fritz's Freudian analysis, there were certain issues which never really came up.

DR: What do you think Fritz took from his Reichian work that was useful in the development of Gestalt therapy?

LP: The whole concept of character as defense mechanism. We were really both influenced at the time by *Character Analysis*, which Reich had published just at the time when Fritz was in analysis with him.

DR: Gestalt doesn't talk much about character, I think.

LP: Character is a fixed gestalt. And there we use the Reichian concept of the muscular fixations.

DR: I'm thinking about style which is also a fixed gestalt. Gestalt therapists talk much more about style.

LP: Style is something that develops A style is something different. Style is a more integrated way of functioning, of behaving and expressing.

DR: But it can also become a fixed gestalt.

DR: Well, when you say character is a fixed gestalt, it's not something that doesn't develop too, and then become fixed. There has to be a development that rigidifies there.

LP: Usually there are fixations, points where this particular type of restriction or restraint, repression, fixation, was support for something. Any resistance is originally acquired as assistance for something.

DR: You mentioned the concept of character that Reich developed. What about the body armor? Clenching and tightening?

LP: That is the support system for the character. That somebody has character means he has very definite ways of behaving, of expressing, functioning.

DR: I'm trying to differentiate between a mental character and a physical character.

LP: They are the identity. One goes with the other. And if you can fix, can focus immediately in therapy, on the actual tensions and fixations, the mental side of it comes out. By starting with what I can see immediately in the way of tensions and fixations and making them immediately plausible and experiential to the client, I can get through in following that up to the very central conflict.

DR: But it seems to me that you've moved away from character in that way, not that I'm objecting, but I think that may be one of the advantages Gestalt therapy offers. By focusing on what's immediate we don't have to make those kinds of formulations.

LP: The character means that all the fixations which support the character become the work in the ongoing gestalt formulation.

DR: Well, would you say that Gestalt by focusing on the immediate tensions and working with them then doesn't get as involved with what the larger character formation would be, because those either unravel or reform or become integrated so that...Reich, on the one hand has all these diagnostic pictures of this heavy psychoanalytically oriented theoretical machinery, in Gestalt therapy...

LP: I don't think it's necessary at all. Actually, what we are trying to do in Gestalt therapy is to bring into the foreground again the fixations which have become kind of petrified and just states of existencewhere so they can be experienced as actual activity that is still done now because it's all the voluntary muscles that are involved. If you can say, "I am tensing. I am stiffening. I am stopping myself breathing," you then can experiment with alternatives. Then, very often, the memories come up. Original experiences to fix oneself in a certain way.

DR: What of Freud's theory of recapturing the memory and then living it through again and then going on?

LP: If you get the memories in interpretation of dreams and of fantasies and you still have the muscular fixations, you can't do very much with it. You either believe the interpretation and you introject it. Or you don't, you reject it and then smother it. So, very often the premature interpretation, the interpretation which the therapist gives, leads to what Freud already called the negative therapeutic reaction. Actually, in identifying with the activity of his resistance, the client can make his own interpretation. It becomes immediate experience.

DR: That's another fruitful aspect of Gestalt therapy that I've always wondered about and am interested in how it was developed: A recognition of the resistance as a creative part of the personality.

LP: It originally was assistance for something. And what does it assist? What is it good for? What does it do for you? Or what did it do, perhaps, for you at one time and now doesn't do?

DR: Whose concept was that? How did it develop? Can you remember that? The creative nature of resistance and the way of working with it. I think, is one of the revolutionary aspects of treatment in Gestalt therapy.

LP: I don't really remember. The work was so continually communicated between us that I can't possibly remember who thought what first.

DR: When you say, "the work between us," who is the "us"?

LP: First it was Fritz and me in South Africa, with *Ego, Hunger and Aggression*, where I collaborated on everything.

DR: In those days what kind of communication was there between you? Was it over the dinner table, or breakfast, or pillow talk, or what?

LP: It was mainly weekend work, because Fritz was in the army during the years when we worked on *Ego, Hunger and Aggression*. He was stationed at the military hospital at Potchefstroom about thirty miles from Johannesburg. He was talking over his ideas with his colleagues there and we discussed them over his weekends at home. Also, there was another friend of ours involved, a Dutch journalist and writer who became our closest friend and who helped us with the English because Fritz's written English was not good at all. He knew English before I did and he could speak it better than I, but I got into the writing of it much more quickly.

DR: Who was your Dutch friend?

LP: His name was Hugo Posthumous, but his nickname was Jumbo and that's how he was known amongst our circle. He was very bright and interesting man who spoke seven languages.

DR: You've mentioned some other people there who were influential in the development of the ideas set forth in *Ego, Hunger, and Aggression*.

LP: Smuts's, *Holism and Evolution*. At the time Fritz was very impressed by him. He met Smuts once or twice and Smuts actually had promised to write an introduction for

Ego, Hunger, and Aggression, but then when the war broke out he had no time any more, of course. So we had to do without it.

DR: In *Ego, Hunger, and Aggression* you used the term "concentration therapy"?

LP: We called it "concentration" therapy as against the "association" therapy.

DR: So that was more a technique focus.

LP: Yes. It's what Gendlin now would call focusing.

DR: It also always seems to be part of the awareness continuum too. Pick something that you would come to and stay with it, rather than to just keep associating. Letting awareness develop and then concentrating.

LP: The awareness continuum is very often mistaken now in Gestalt therapy and people say they practice the awareness continuum when that can be just a kind of free association or a free dissociation, hopping from one thing to another. Now I'm aware of this. Now I'm aware of that. Actually, the awareness continuum develops when you remove or dissolve the barricades, the muscular tensions, the interferences, the fixed gestalt. You concentrate on the fixed gestalten and how you fix them.

DR: When I heard some of Fritz's tapes at Esalen, it seemed to me he was practicing the way you just mentioned.

LP: Yes, I think that's a mistake and that Fritz was much more analytically oriented than he realized. I think that the hot seat, empty chair and the directing of the patient to his own interpretation is a kind of dramatized free association.

DR: In a sense he had come back with the empty chair and the hot seat to the couch with the therapist behind.

LP: As a result he would keep himself out and only give certain directions or orders. That came partly from his pre-psychiatric theater experience for several years at the Reinhardt School.

DR: And he was mainly working with projection as a major means of treating people.

LP: You can work this way with comparatively healthy people, but you can't work with the empty chair method with really very sick people. He stopped really treating people. In the workshops, he was working with people who were all professionals — mostly advanced professionals who had already been in practice for several years, or had their own therapists or analysts already. He simply bypassed people when he felt that they were not safe. Fritz was a generator but not a nourisher. Fritz had wonderful ideas and intuitions, but no patience.

DR: You mentioned the early work in New York. Who were the most important people?

LP: For me, Paul Goodman was the most important because he was the only one who stimulated me in directions that I hadn't gone before.

DR: Give me an example.

LP: He was a Renaissance man, one of the very few that were made in America. Here people usually don't have the education and background where they know languages, and philosophies, and different ways of thinking, and art, and anthropology, and music. Paul had all of that along with integrated functioning.

DR: He developed some of that when he was working with you as a patient.

LP: He developed a different style. He developed a style of communication which before therapy with me was harder, aggressive and rebellious. After our work together, he became more grounded.

DR: What was his contribution to you?

LP: His therapy developed gradually into a kind of mutual therapy. And I got as much from him.

DR: What?

LP: More confidence in myself and more independence in my own thinking.

DR: What was it like, being Mrs. Fritz Perls, in a way?

LP: I had to cope with this for many years. I remember an incident in South Africa where I had met the editor of a Sunday newspaper and he said he would like to get an interview with me. He sent an interviewer and a photographer and their first question was "What is it like to be the wife of a psychoanalyst?" I couldn't really tell them because I'm a psychoanalyst myself and they quickly packed their stuff and left. It was tough to be married to Fritz. Not in the beginning. Not for many years. It became difficult when we were here. In South Africa it wasn't difficult. In South Africa he needed me, you see, because there was nobody who had a relevant background for which he worked and thought. Later there were many people who influenced him and in our later years we lived apart most of the time. In South Africa, we had similar backgrounds and worked out our ideas together. He had no one with whom he could relevantly discuss our work. There were very few people. There were some people who trained with us, who were well read, but they didn't have the experience.

DR: Fritz was well trained as a physician...

LP: No, Fritz was not well trained as a physician. Fritz was war trained. He went into the army before he finished his training and when he came back from the war all the medical students were quickly pushed through their later courses and their residencies. He immediately got involved in psychoanalysis without having a good medical background.

DR: And your background was more in philosophy and psychology?

LP: I immediately went into Gestalt psychology. That is what seduced me away from law and economics. I was hearing lectures by Gelp when I was still studying law. He was a very good lecturer. He was interesting. He was literate. He had an entirely different focus from the traditional psychologists. Later I was more impressed by Wertheimer and by Goldstein. As a lecturer and an introduction to Gestalt, Gelp was excellent, but he was very difficult as a supervisor for my dissertation.

DR: What led you toward psychoanalysis?

LP: Fritz. I got into psychoanalysis because I wanted to understand the jargon that he and another friend used all the time and to get an idea of what they were talking about. They were wildly analyzing everybody around, including me. And I wanted in.

DR: How did you get in?

LP: Fritz was in analysis with Clara Happle, who was a Freudian analyst trained in Berlin and I went into analysis with her too.

DR: How long were you with her and what was it like?

LP: I was with her only about six months, perhaps a little longer. Then she moved to Hamburg so I went to Carl Landauer who was *the* analyst at the time.

DR: What was your experience as a patient in psychoanalysis?

LP: I was much more impressed with Landauer who was extraordinarily bright and liberal within the psychoanalytic area. He was a close friend of Ferenzi and Groddeck, who were already on the fringes. More independent, more active, actually.

DR: I want to go back and ask you to explore politics and art. What influence did they have on you and on the development of Gestalt therapy?

LP: At the time we were quite involved in left-wing politics. In South Africa most people in our circle had been involved in that. Some of our South African friends were very involved with the Fourth International and they asked me why I wasn't more politically active. I said, "You know, I think the work that I am doing is political work. If you work with people to get them to the point where they can think on their own and sort themselves out from the majority confluences, it's political work and it radiates even if we can work only with a very limited number of people. We choose the kind of people to work with, who again have influence on others. That is political work."

DR: You mentioned Paul Goodman and talked of reading him in *Politics*. Dwight McDonald [the editor and publisher of *Politics*] was an anarchist and Paul was an anarchist.

LP: Gestalt therapy is an anarchistic process in the sense that it doesn't conform to pre-set rules and regulations. It doesn't try to adjust people into a certain system, but rather to adjust them to their own creative potential.

DR: You've often said Gestalt is not an adjustment therapy. I took that to mean that when each person is finding a way for his own gestalts to emerge and to take those...

LP: But he doesn't emerge within empty space. He is always surrounded by whatever happens to be the case.

DR: The field. Contact with what's there at this moment. But that already suggests a kind of unconventional, non-conservative, hip approach to the individual and society.

LP: The conservative attitude is to a great extent based on very fixed gestalt. I'm thinking of a verse by Goethe:

Es erben sich Gesetz' und Rechte
Wie eine ew'ge Krankheit fort...

[Although Laura proceeds to translate the third line, she does not quote it in the interview: "Vernunft wird Unsinn, Wohltat plage..." It is from *Faust, Part I.*]

DR: You have to translate that for me.

LP: "Law and right are inherited like a disease, an eternal disease where wrong becomes right and right becomes wrong." [Laura's translation captures the spirit of Geothe's words, but her translation is somewhat inaccurate.]

DR: So it's a political act to be doing therapy.

LP: Any therapy, or anything one does in a concentrated way with people is a political act. Starting with teaching, or even in the family with the ordinary, traditional ways of upbringing.

DR: In *Ego, Hunger and Aggression* and in some of *Gestalt Therapy* there are direct links to the larger social system and to the wider culture.

LP: It is through Fritz's personal influence, particularly on the West Coast, and through his extended work all over the world that focusing on the individual has become so absolutely prevalent. And, of course, it was taken up very eagerly at the time, because a lot of people — young people particularly — were disillusioned with the social attitudes of the times. Others were objecting to the [Vietnam] war.

DR: Well, what do you think about Gestalt therapy becoming an introject?

LP: I'm trying to work against that wherever I can. Gestalt therapy is in danger of becoming a fixed gestalt, particularly here [by "here," Laura means North America].

DR: Literature has certainly been important to you and you've written short stories and poems. Paul Goodman wrote plays and novels and short stories and poems.

LP: A work of art is always an integration of previously different and diverse and partly incompatible parts into a new whole in which they make sense and that can be in a mathematical formula, or it can be a poem or a story, or it can be a dance, or...

DR: Well, let me play sociologist. Let us say if we take the background of the people who were first important in the development of Gestalt therapy, there weren't many mathematicians and there weren't many cooks.

LP: No.

DR: There were more artists and writers. Here's my private agenda that I'm going to force into your interview. I was always impressed with Fritz, his own background in the theater, his interest in opera, Paul's interest in writing and literature and drama, your own interest in music and literature. And the three of you being so essential to the development of Gestalt therapy. And that although you didn't start out as a group of artists to create a therapeutic technique, the background in art was so important.

LP: Therapy is also an art. It's more of an art than it is a science. It takes a lot of intuition and sensitivity and an overall view means something very different from a piecemeal association approach. Being an artist is functioning holistically. And being a good therapist also means that.

DR: Do you want to say something about Paul Weisz now? [Paul Weisz was one of the original members of The New York Institute for Gestalt Therapy and was, along with Laura, Fritz, Paul Goodman and Isadore From, an original trainer of the Cleveland group that was the founding basis for the Gestalt Institute of Cleveland. Of the early group, Weisz was the most interested in Zen and was responsible for the influence of eastern philosophies on Gestalt therapy.]

LP: Paul Weisz was a European.

DR: And you mean by that...

LP: I mean by that that he had, educationally, a similar background. Which means humanistic education. Which

Fritz, by the way also had, but he disowned it in some way. His schools were not as good as mine were. He had no respect for the teachers. He was bored. He was stuck three times in the same class. Which is really a superior work of spite.

DR: When was he held back?

LP: When he was fifteen, sixteen, something like that. The years from thirteen to sixteen I think he was just stuck.

DR: Still at the height of his adolescence.

LP: They took him out of school and put him into business, which was even worse. Then he chose another school that he went through then with flying colors.

DR: Well, you were talking about what it means to be a European and about Paul Weisz.

LP: It meant having a much wider and deeper background in language, in everything. In everything that you can find here if you are lucky in college, when they are already interested in girls and in cars and in what to do with their lives. We started learning languages, starting with Latin and Greek when we were nine or ten, along with science, mathematics, and history. Not only German history. What I got in school was only a jumping off point to go in all kinds of directions, reading in many subjects.

DR: You mentioned Tillich and Buber earlier.

LP: Tillich and Buber were much more than what one usually thinks of as theologians. They were really psychologists.

DR: What is the difference?

LP: They were interested in people, they were not talking about subjects. Listening to Tillich or Buber, you felt they were talking directly to you and not just about some *thing*. The kind of contact they made was essential in their theories.

DR: Can you talk about the difference between Germany, South Africa, New York, and California?

LP: When I came to New York I had no time, really, to find out what it was like and how it was different. I had to acclimatize very quickly. I had first to get my children acclimatized and find schools for them and to find a place to live. I started practicing immediately. When we first arrived Fritz wanted to show us everything and took us immediately to Times Square and to Gimbels and Macy's. It was just horrifying. Fritz had made contact with some artists and was also already writing with Paul. Through Paul we made contact with Paul McDonald [Laura is probably referring to Dwight McDonald, noted critic and publisher of the magazine *Politics* in the late '40s and '50s]. I immediately got into a circuit where I felt very much at home.

DR: If you were to compare Berlin in the 30's and New York in the late '40s and '50s, what similarities and what differences were there?

LP: It was different in many ways. In Berlin one was already sitting on a wake. And I didn't get that feeling here. In a way the ivory tower here was much safer.

DR: What about the differences?

LP: But I found a lot of difference in the way I was taken as a female intellectual. Actually everywhere — in South Africa, and in Germany, and here — I was always one of the boys. But in Germany and in Europe it's all a cartoon to a great extent. The boys didn't really forget that I was a woman too. But they forgot it somehow here. I remember, I was at a party with Paul Goodman somewhere on Ninth Avenue — a dingy neighborhood. It was one o'clock in the morning. I wanted to go home, and he said, "Oh, I'll walk you to your bus." We walked together to what I suppose was Eighth Avenue. And we stood there for a while. And a bus came in the other direction from where I had to go. And Paul said, "Oh, there is my bus," and he hopped on the bus. And I'm standing there. At one o'clock in the morning in that neighborhood. It wouldn't have happened in Germany. But he didn't think of me, really, as a woman who possibly had to be protected.

DR: What else influenced the development of Gestalt therapy?

LP: We all took from Eastern philosophies and their holistic approach.

DR: When you say "Eastern philosophy" you mean, more specifically?

LP: Buddhism and Eastern literature in translation. When I was a young girl, an Indian poet was giving recitals all over and we read him. Hermann Hesse was writing at the same time and we got his works fresh from the presses. Later I read *Zen and the Art of Archery*. I had also from the East the exercises — the modern dance movements which are to a very great extent based much more on Eastern attitudes and movements than on what has been developed in the West, namely ballet — which is no support for anything but is something like coloratura singing and can be very beautiful in itself.

DR: Would you say your use of your body or your breathing...

LP: It's not the use of the body. This is already a piecemeal attitude. You are up here in your head and you have a body somewhere down there. Actually the point is to be a body. This is something that I make clear in every workshop and in all of my groups: that when you are a body, when you experience yourself totally as a body, then you are *somebody*. Language knows what it is talking about. And when you don't have that, you very easily experience yourself as *nobody*.

This conversation, originally recorded on videotape in the spring of 1984, was edited for publication by Joe Wysong. It first appeared in Volume XIV, Number 1, (spring, 1991) of *The Gestalt Journal*. The interview was conducted by Daniel Rosenblatt, a long time friend and professional associate of Dr. Perls.

2.

An Anniversary Talk

My dear friends, I may call all of you that who have come here tonight to celebrate with us the 25th anniversary of the New York Institute for Gestalt Therapy.

This is a joyous occasion, especially for me, seeing what started 25 years ago as a far out, daring experiment involving only a handful of people, of dedicated people, and a small number of higglety-pigglety assembled students and clients, now fully grown into an ever developing, comprehensive method of therapy that is being taught and practiced not only in the United States but in most parts of the world.

I don't want to bore you with a long lecture on the beginnings and the developments of our Institute, but I would like to share with you some of the memories of the people who were involved at the time when we started.

Four people that Fritz and I had been working with already for a few years joined us as teachers at the start of the Institute. They were: Paul Goodman, Paul Weisz, Elliott Shapiro, and Isadore From.

Paul Goodman's contribution to Gestalt therapy is still widely underestimated. Actually there would not be any coherent theory of Gestalt therapy without him. The second part of *Gestalt Therapy: Excitement and Growth in the Human Personality* is largely his work and luckily we have now his collected psychological essays which reflect his development as a therapist, as a theorist, and Gestalt therapist. For us who worked with him and were his friends, Paul has remained a living presence and we celebrate him on this day of remembrance.

Paul Weisz was, like Paul Goodman, a born teacher, producing, apparently without effort, observations, ideas, theories, and jokes from an inexhaustible background of experience, knowledge, and imagination ranging from alchemy to biochemistry, from ecology to mathematics, from fairy tales to philosophy, from Cabala to Zen Buddhism. If he did any writing, and I have the suspicion that he did, he did not publish anything. And as he also died much too early, he lives unforgettably in the memory of those who had the great good fortune to work with him — his patients and his students here in New York and in Cleveland, and his friends.

And there is Elliott Shapiro who did the first Gestalt courses for educators, but stayed with the Institute only a few years before he became so fully involved and immersed in the problems of innovative education and educational politics that there was no time and energy left for us. But he is alive and well.

Ralph Hefferline who was a co-author of *Gestalt Therapy: Excitement and Growth* did not join the staff of the Institute. At the time a close association with us probably did not fit in with his academic career. He did a few guest lectures and stayed in contact, even if only through sending patients and students right up to the year until his premature death.

Of the original founders, only two are still alive and active in the Institute, Isadore From and I. Isadore started with the course that he announced as "not being given this year," but since then he has given a lot of practica and seminars, worked with innumerable patients, trained a great number of therapists, here in New York and in Cleveland, and has become our finest therapist and teacher. Today we honor him as an ever more creative and delightful, faithful old friend and collaborator. And we also celebrate his sixtieth birthday, which he had last month.

It is not easy to talk about Fritz's role in the development of the Institute. At least it's not easy for me. He was the most interested one in starting it and gave the introductory lectures and part of the workshops for a number of years. Fritz's genius was in his intuitive insights and uncanny hunches, which then would have to be substantiated in more exact elaboration. Fritz very often did not have the patience for this detailed work. He was a generator, not a developer or an organizer. Without the constant support from his friends, and from me, without the constant encouragement and collaboration,

Fritz would never have written a line, nor founded any-thing. But he had the kind of charismatic personality that could easily involve people in his ideas and plans and get them to take care quite enthusiastically of all the details that he himself did not like to bother about.

In this context, I want to mention, besides the people who became teachers, Jim Hoffman, who as the Institute's secretary took care of all the technicalities like publicity, printing and mailing of brochures and course admission cards, etc., etc. I, in particular, came to appre-ciate his work, for when he could not do it any more I became the Jack of all trades. I took all the phone calls and referral interviews and I answered the mail. Every-thing took place in my house — all the workshops and meetings. Besides Fritz and myself, Isadore and Paul Weiss had their offices in our house too.

When the idea of starting an institute for Gestalt therapy was hatched between Fritz and Paul Goodman after the publication of *Gestalt Therapy: Excitement and Growth*, I made it clear that I was not going to take any part in it. On top of an ever increasing practice I had a house, children and grandchildren, and did not feel like taking on any additional responsibilities. I also was used mainly to individual work. I had worked with a small group only for a couple of years and was still scared of working with larger groups.

But at Fritz's first lecture forty people turned up. So for the practicum, he took twenty and I took twenty. And here I still am.

I want to say something about the people who came to the institute as patients and trainees. Through the thousands of brochures which we sent out to all professionals in and around New York, we got almost no response. The people who joined were either our patients or Paul Goodman's friends. From there developed long chains of personal and professional referrals out of Columbia, Yeshiva, and Adelphi Universities, from Kings County, Bellevue, and St. Luke's Hospitals, from the Veteran's Administration and other institutions.

Nearly all the people who are now our trainers worked with us in the first ten years. Most of them started as patients who in spite of, or perhaps because of, their many talents and interests could not find a congenial place in our tightly structured society. They found through and in Gestalt therapy not only a professional — but a vocation.

So for many years we did not advertise, but developed very quietly as a membership organization that functioned on an apprenticeship system, minimally organized but steadily growing. It is only in the last few years that, due to the increasing popularity of Gestalt therapy and our growing membership, we had to organize in a somewhat more structured way and we are continually re-thinking our process. It is extremely difficult not to fall into the trap of a fixed Gestalt and to remain on the growing edge.

In the later fifties and early sixties, the cultural climate started to change. I believe that the Gestalt approach, particularly Fritz's work in many places and Paul Goodman's writings — *Growing Up Absurd, Compulsory Mis-Education* and others — substantially contributed to this humanistic development. Not only in therapy and education, but in the total lifestyle of a younger generation. But if Fritz and Paul were the sorcerers, their true disciples were and are frequently sorcerer's apprentices who never fully understood the realistic and organismic fundamentals of Gestalt therapy, but unleashed a flood of anti-intellectualism, forgetting that it is the intellect that makes us different from other living creatures. It is the specifically *human* equipment. By dismissing any intellectual discourse as "bullshit," the practice of Gestalt therapy becomes impoverished and simplistic and is, in fact, not being taken seriously by many serious therapists and teachers who have been exposed only to this one-sided and diminished approach. But I'm happy to see in the last couple of years a growing recognition of this mindlessness in present day humanism, and I take some credit for my contribution to this change through my work with many groups in the States and all over Europe.

I don't want to end without expressing my gratitude to some people who from the beginning showed interest and even confidence in our enterprise. There is, first, Arthur Ceppos, of Julian Press, who took the risk of publishing, in 1951, *Gestalt Therapy: Excitement and Growth in the Human Personality*. He said, at the time, this book will go very slowly at first, and in ten years it will be a classic. He was right. It has become our Bible.

But right away it got some people outside New York interested. In a ten-day intensive course three people from Cleveland turned up, among them Erv Polster, who has become one of the foremost exponents of Gestalt therapy. They started, in 1953, the Cleveland

Gestalt Institute, which has developed into an active and many-faceted Gestalt institute.

There is Bill Groman, now a professor of psychology in Richmond, Virginia, who has trained and supervised most of the Washington, D.C., Gestalt people — who in the early fifties went back to college and through the years of academic studies in order to become a Gestalt therapist.

The first opportunity to take part in an interdisciplinary symposium was provided by Sam and Karen McGruval. Prodded probably by Leo Chafin and Ira Suldillano for their case reports in clinical psychology at Kings County Hospital. This symposium was chaired by the late Harry Bone. I contributed with two instances of Gestalt therapy. Harry Bone wrote an extraordinarily witty and imaginative discussion in which he had me talk from the Gestalt point of view in a much more poignant way than I myself could have managed at the time. I wish he could have written my speech today.

The next opportunity, this time at a national scale, presented itself several years later, in 1959, when I was invited by the Academy of Psychotherapists to be on a panel with Carl Rogers, Carl Whittaker, Drichos and Julie Nieds at their yearly conference. Since I became a member of A.A.P., I did Gestalt workshops at every summer workshop for more than ten years. It is through the personal contact and the friendships that developed, as much as through Fritz's work in Columbus, Miami, and later on the west coast, that Gestalt therapy became acknowledged as a major therapeutic method and that numbers of patients and trainees were referred to us from all over the States.

I have the pleasure of greeting some A.A.P. members here tonight – some of whom have become members of our Institute or who have started institutes in Atlanta and in Washington.

So have other long established and well-known therapists, coming from very different orientations, joined the Institute: Betsy Mintz, Ruth Cohn, who sent me a long letter and sends her best wishes and congratulations to the Institute and all the members, Leon Menaker and Ruth Ronall, Alan Schwartz, and others.

Finally, I want to thank all the fellows and members who through the years have given workshops and seminars: Isadore From, Richard Kitzler, Pat Kelly, Magda Denes, the late Buck Eastman, Paul Oliver, Daniel Rosenblatt, Marilyn Rosanes, David Altfeld, Karen Humphrey, Elaine Rapp, Theo Skolnik, and many others.

And last but not least, I thank all the co-workers who, in the last few years, have relieved me of all the duties and chores which for many years I had taken on myself. In particular, the successive vice presidents: Isadore From, Daniel Rosenblatt, Richard Kitzler, and Jean Greggs. I thank the people who took care of finances and other time consuming services: Marilyn Rosanes, Doug Davidove, Art Bartunek. All the members who took turns in answering inquiries, interviewing and referring potential patients and trainees, and all those members and associates who are, or have been, on the executive board and all of you who are involved in the activities of the Institute and so are supporting its ongoing development.

And now I wish all of you, all of us, a very happy evening. Enjoy yourselves and each other.

Thank you.

This talk was written by Laura Perls who read it at the 25th Anniversary Dinner of The New York Institute for Gestalt Therapy. It originally appeared in Volume XIII, Number 2, (fall, 1990) of *The Gestalt Journal.*

Section II

THEORY

3.

How to Educate Children for Peace

Confronted with the question: "How can we educate children for peace?" the psychoanalyst finds herself in a difficult position. Psychoanalysts look at human beings and their behavior not moralistically but psychologically. We try to see things as they are, not as they should be. And so, before we can suggest anything about how to train children for peace, we first have to state the conditions and possibilities which this task presents. Perhaps we also shall have to destroy some delusions, which many people suffer from because they put their own wishes before facts.

I want to draw your attention in particular to the fact that the demand for peace is in strict opposition to one of the most vital instincts of every living being, namely *aggression*.

By "aggression" most people understand the wish to attack, to destroy and to kill. Therefore they condemn it wholeheartedly, and the general trend in our civilization for many centuries goes towards the more or less complete suppression of this apparently most dangerous instinct.

As we all ought to know, the small child is a little savage, an untamed animal, whose behavior is directed primarily by the pleasure principle and with little thought to the demands of reality. The steps by which the child is taught the demands of reality vary in different homes. Usually the average family reacts in the following way: Every overt sign of aggression in the child (crying, kicking, biting, breaking things, etc.) is met by the grown ups with disapproval. The same disapproval is directed at the child's impatience and bad moods. His outbreaks of temper often lead to severe punishment. The conscientious parent tries to realize his ideal of a good citizen — which he usually can't fulfill himself — in his children. The child is told to be good natured, obedient, respectful. This aim is usually achieved either by appealing to the child's fear of trouble and punishment or to his desire to be loved.

One might expect that people who have been trained from the beginning of their lives to be considerate of their neighbors, to respect property, to obey authority, would have the best possible training for peace. But if we look today at the countries where for hundreds of generations people have been brought up in this way, we must admit that the results are rather disappointing. Wherever we look, we see people engaging in or preparing for war,

young people enthusiastic about going to war and philoso-
phers seeking to find justifications to prove the necessity
of wars — all this in spite of religious and humanitarian
ideals. How can we understand this?

First, in order to find out, we have to scrutinize the
common conception of "aggression." This conception is
mainly derived from the effects which aggression has on
the people exposed to it. The small child's aggression
causes grown ups a lot of inconvenience and annoyance.
Therefore most people regard it as undesirable and try to
break the child's will. But they are in danger of not only
suppressing his so-called "naughtiness," his crying and
shouting, biting, kicking and scratching, tearing and
breaking things, but also of suppressing his curiosity and
his inquisitiveness. Of course, the child's inquisitiveness
and his physical aggressiveness are very trying for the
grown ups. Their satisfaction demands so much time and
patience, and they can be very embarrassing. They even
call for the admission of one's own ignorance, which
many parents regard as serious damage to their authority.
But on the other hand curiosity and inquisitiveness are
indispensable conditions for the child's intellectual development, his capacity to learn and to study, to understand
people and circumstances. And complete suppression of
aggressiveness causes — if not stupidity, then certainly
serious intellectual inhibition — and leads to the impossi-
bility of critical thinking. Within the family that may
appear as an asset. The parents' demand for respect
implies that the child should not question the grown ups,
that one should do as one is told, that one should believe
what one is taught, in general that one should be accept-

ing and not critical. The psychologist concludes meta-
phorically that a lot is forced down a child's throat,
without permission to bite or to chew or to digest. In
fact, that is not just a convenient metaphor but the possibility to bite, to chew, to digest and to assimilate physical
food (and on the other side the power to think, to criticize, to understand which represents the means to assimilate intellectual food) are only differentiations of the same
aggressive instinct. Our psychoanalytical experience
shows that the suppression of the one side very seriously
affects the other side and vice versa.

I prefer not to enter into a lengthy technical
discussion of the problem. If you understand what an
important part the aggressive instinct plays in a child's
development, you can certainly recognize that the consequences of our traditional upbringing are usually disastrous.

People who have been brought up toward blind
obedience, who can't think and act independently, using
their own insight and will — such people can only do
what they are told, and fall an easy prey to anybody who
assumes leadership. These people will believe and accept
anything that is impressed upon them with sufficient
pressure, either with promises or by force. As they have
not trained their capacity for criticism, they have little
possibility to understand social and political circumstances
or to act according to their insight and judgment. They
are easily overwhelmed by a display of apparent strength
and succumb to propaganda. In this way we can explain
the fact that fascism could gain such a large number of
followers in such a short time, not only in the countries

where it originated, but over the whole world, in countries which differ very widely in their historical development, their political system, their national character, or their social and cultural background.

Of course, intellectual immaturity is caused not only by the suppression of early infantile aggression. Of equal importance for development of fascism is the fact that the repression of *individual* aggression usually brings about an increase of *universal* aggression. In all highly civilized countries we can see where the average individual has not developed his aggressive capacities to any considerable extent, but is on the contrary rather restrained, well-behaved, even afraid of complications, that the community has developed its means of aggression into absolutely terrifying extremes. The improvement of the war machinery (guns, tanks, aircraft, bombs, poison gas, military training and strategic efficiency) seems to be in direct proportion to the suppression of individual aggressiveness, as if the repressed aggression of all the individuals had been accumulated into something beyond the individual and simply had to force its way out.

Here we are quite near the truth. Actually an *instinct* cannot be repressed, only its expressions. The aggressive energies remain the same and have to find an outlet. In some cases they may become invested in the resistance *against* aggression, and build a strong conscience, as a means of directing these energies.

Frequently the repressed aggressive energies come out in two most undesirable phenomena: neurosis and delinquency. And in a certain sense these are both foundation pillars for militarism and fascism. That a government, a general, or a "Fuehrer" takes responsibility from the individual's shoulders has an effect like the lid being taken from a kettle of boiling water. Like compressed steam the long repressed and accumulated aggression simply shoots out. But because it was so fully repressed, it could not be transformed in any way, it is still the original aggressiveness of the small child: unintelligent, cruel, bestial — only performed now with the physical strength and the technical means of the grownup. The permission in war or in similar circumstances to commit actions which, under normal circumstances would bring about the social and legal condemnation of the individual, actually means an undoing, an annihilation of the early infantile inhibitions of aggression. And the person or the system which gives this permission, takes the place of the early infantile authorities: father, mother, teachers, etc. But if these authorities *imposed* inhibitions and therefore perhaps met with a certain resentment and fear, the authority which *undoes* these inhibitions is accepted without reserve; he is welcomed as a liberator and a saviour; he is the *good* father, and the fixation which is created may be equally strong or even stronger than the early infantile fixations.

I have painted a rather gloomy picture. I am afraid that it was not quite what you expected, and that I may even have created the impression that I have "gone off the rail" and digressed. To return to our theme: How can we train our children for peace?, *in spite* or perhaps *with* the facts which I have presented.

Our first step must be that we revise our conception of "aggression." Aggression is not only a destructive energy, but the force which is behind all our activities, without which we could not do anything. Aggression not only makes us attack, it also makes us tackle things; it does not only destroy, it also builds up; it not only makes us steal and rob, it also lies behind our endeavors to take hold and to master what we have a right to.

It is a false question whether to repress or not to repress aggression. Since aggression is an indispensable ingredient of human makeup, we have to use it, to develop it into a valuable instrument for the management of our lives. That implies that in particular one should not hamper the very first signs of aggression in the small child, but that one rather should encourage it and provide adequate support for it. In the beginning that means mainly sufficient food, as a lack usually creates greediness. As soon as the child's teeth begin to grow, he wants to bite. Now he needs solid food and toys. Otherwise he will bite just what he can get hold of, even mother's finger or breast; but if he does it, it should not be regarded as a crime. Later on, toys should be something that the child can work with: blocks, sand, clay, paper, crayons, etc. They should stimulate the child's creative and constructive abilities. Toys which only can be spoiled or destroyed, without providing material for new activities, are of limited use. Where the parents have a pacifistic attitude, they probably won't give their children any militaristic toys: guns, soldiers, etc. But even if they do, I don't think that the child will suffer for his whole life through their rather superficial influences, if in general he has learned to think and act independently.

And so I come again to the point, which I want to emphasize most strongly: Mothers — and fathers — should encourage the child's mental activities from the very beginning. Children should be allowed to find things out, even if that occasionally would mean breaking a doll and finding out what is inside. Children's questions should be answered as honestly as possible. Although the child knows little, his curiosity and his inquisitiveness are his major means by which he can gain knowledge and experience. If he is told: "Don't be silly!", if he is made to feel that he is too small and too young to understand things and that he only stands in the way of the big people when they work or amuse themselves, he will not be able to get rid of this feeling of inferiority when he is himself grown up. The child is concerned with the present and keeps his earliest reactions to his environment as a pattern for his future life. He will then regard his own opinions and his own achievements as small and unimportant in comparison with other people's, he will perhaps not even try to do anything of his own accord or to think his own thoughts, but he will just do and believe as he is told. And that means that as a social and political being he will be a very doubtful quality, he will be unintelligent and unreliable. But a child who has not repressed his aggression, who has learned to make use of it, to manage it, will later be able to take an *intelligent* part in social and political life.

"How to Educate Children for Peace" was written in German and published in Johannesburg, South Africa, in 1939. It has been edited for publication by Joe Wysong. This is its first publication in English.

4.

Notes on the Mythology of Suffering and Sex

I.

When the "Missing Link" left the last tree, the tree of knowledge, and walked away on his two legs — leaving the burning forests behind — Adam, becoming human, had committed his act of original sin. Driven out of Paradise, he and all his kin were condemned to lifelong labor and final death.

The Biblical myth, accepted through the ages as the true story of the first human being, must represent an adequate symbolization of Man as he found himself at the very beginning of his human development. Moreover, the persistence and validity of the myth have been guaranteed by the earliest experience of every man in the beginning of his individual life. Driven out of the intra-uterine paradise, every man has to face the tribulations of his own separate existence and the continuous threat of his own inevitable personal death.

During the last few centuries, the Biblical myths have lost some of their original validity. Their apparent incongruity with the results of scientific research has led to their conscious abandonment by the more rationally minded. But the concepts of "original sin" or "the curse of labor and death" still permeate contemporary existence, the former embedded in the *a priori* guilt feeling which demands a continuous effort at justification of our existence, the latter in the all-pervading hopelessness and indifference, which has taken the place of the rationally untenable expectation of a compensating life hereafter. This hopelessness seems to me not — as is commonly thought — a result of, but rather a condition for, our present-day political and economic circumstances. Over-industrialization, war and the atomic bomb provide a convenient projection screen for the unrealized misinterpretation of the human condition as it exists today.

In the Western cultures, there is as yet no valid myth which could take the place of the old, obsolete ones and give that facilitation for human development and guidance for human conduct which science and technology alone are unable to afford. Yet a myth cannot be invented *ad hoc*; it grows out of the unconscious realization of the human position and affects the unconscious layers of the personality, e.g., the automatic behavior, even long after its manifest content has been consciously rejected or "scientifically explained." At this point, we can only try to de-automatize the obsolete traditional attitudes, to debunk and re-interpret the old myths, to discover and integrate the forces and potentialities which have been prevented from being realized not only in the neurotic individual, but in the whole human species. We must clear the ground for the growth of a new myth, which could strengthen and guide humanity in the period of its development that it is entering now, and give human existence a meaning adequate to this development. The Biblical myths of Adam's Fall and the Passion of Christ could give this meaning and guidance through many centuries, but the merely scientific theories of Marx and Freud or the philosophy of Nietzsche could not, even for a few decades. In the *conscious* elaboration of a scientific or political theory into a myth, the scientific ground soon is lost, and what remains is pseudo-science and pseudo-myth: the totalitarian monstrosities of Hitlerism and Stalinism.

II.

It is customary to give the legend of Adam and Eve a sexual-*moral* interpretation; temptation and seduction, disobedience and punishment are its main ingredients. But for a legend to become a valid myth, the rational moral issue is not forceful enough. To give direction to human development for millennia to come, it must be deeply anchored in the biological.

The sexual interpretation of the legend seems strangely inadequate to account for the validity of the myth. Paradoxically, it presents as sinful, what is the least possible break in the paradisial confluence. Adam "knew" Eve, he became aware of the difference of the sexes, of her "otherness." But at the height of the sexual orgasm this awareness of difference is lost again; Man experiences himself as completely involved in a natural process, not just part of it, but "it": "and they shall be one flesh." Every single sexual act, if carried to its conclusion, carries with it the expiation of the crime of recognition and alienation.

Thus the sexual interpretation of the legend appears to be premature, and its continuation into a myth an obsessional symptom. What originally is felt as a crime is not the sexual aspect, but the actual awareness of difference in the widest sense. The myth of the Fall represents not a "moral" fall from "spiritual" grace (these conceptions would demand an advanced development in abstraction which we cannot possibly expect from Man in the initial stages of his human career) but rather an actual fall of the ape from the tree, coming down on his hind legs and having to let go the once protective hanging-on grip on the now burning tree. Of course, we can look at the "burning forests" theory as just another myth. This would not discredit, but rather confirm its validity, if not historically, certainly physiologically. For whatever is experienced as different is exciting, "burning." Man is no more part of the tree, but suddenly aware of himself as different, apart, alone. And in the very beginning of his development, Man does not experience this otherness as "standing up" or "independence," but as "fall" and "being cast out." He is not aware of his equipment for discrimination and judgment as his own, but projects it onto God and the Angel with the Sword, who guards the closed door to Paradise.

If, as it seems, Man himself erected the barrier to Paradise, we can assume that at the time it must have been, or have appeared to him as, in the interest of his human development. There merely sexual interpretation is in direct support of the barrier, as the uninhibited sex act is the easiest and most obvious return to Paradise (as every healthy human being knows). To safeguard his human development of orientation and manipulation (coping with the other, the different), Man had to get rid of the feeling of guilt that originates in the breaking of confluence on the one hand, in the incomplete awareness and the incompetent handling of difference on the other. He deflected his guilt feelings into the most innocuous channel, sex, where the "knowing," the awareness of difference, is quite unessential and redundant (animals copulate quite effectively without "knowing"), and where the competent handling of the situation need not be "conscious," as the essence of the act is a spontaneous orgastic reflection.

This displacement, or rather narrowing down of the whole issue of awareness to its most insignificant part has the most far-reaching consequences. On the one hand, it guarantees Man's specifically human development, leaving free his curiosity, interest and enterprise for everything else except sex. On the other hand, it is responsible for the most insidious split in the development of human relationship. The limited guilt feeling leaves free the way of objective approach (orientation and manipulation, creativeness, likeness to the image of God) for Man, but it falls heavily on Woman, leaving her far behind in the animal chains of reproduction and child rearing. Woman remains involved in sex, i.e., in sin; she is of the devil, the eternal temptress, contemptible and mysterious (because Man does not want to know her), redeemed only by the birth of sons, who in turn will become Men and justify her existence, while her daughters will barely be tolerated as potential bearers of sons. And while Man gradually alleviates the curse of having to work "by the sweat of his brow" by his own creative imagination, thus changing the world and himself, becoming more and more right, righteous, good, clear, competent, etc., nothing can alleviate Women's burden of unimaginative animal creativity. Until the arrival of electricity and birth control, the demands of domesticity remained substantially the same through the centuries and did not provide much scope for creative imagination. Woman remained inferior, sinister, mysterious, left to cope with the consequences of sin within the limited scope of domesticity, despising herself and envying the male.

Woman's so-called "penis envy" has not much to do with Man's sexual supremacy, but — if it exists at all — is an outcome of the same obsessional attitude that produced the sexual guilt feelings. The penis in this context is not a symbol of sexual superiority, but of everything that is not sexual, e.g., that is not concerned with the continuation of the species, but with the development of the individual, its uniqueness and comparative independence. But, as the term "penis envy" indicates, the obsessional sexual interpretation has permeated even the contemporary psychoanalytical attempts to re-integrate sex into the human fabric. Just as once sex was taken as the source of all evil, now it is regarded as the source of all blessing, the cure-all, and the repression of sex has become the scapegoat.

But we know by now (or at least we should know) that the mere undoing of sexual repression does not re-open the door to Paradise. On the contrary, it brings about what could be called a "negative therapeutic reaction." Without a previous strengthening of the ego functions, the removal of the limited guilt feeling (e.g., of the obsessional safety barrier) simply opens the door to an unlimited guilt feeling concerning all discrimination and differentiation, expressing itself in general desensitization and indifference and, particularly amongst the young, in an all-pervading anti-intellectualism. The mass neurosis of religious sexual repression has been followed by the mass psychosis of industrialism and totalitarianism. Contemporary Man, in his ancient fear of freedom, produces a standardized and uniform mode of living, in which he makes the least and worst possible use of his human equipment for orientation and manipulation.

This contemporary indifference and uniformity has nothing in common with the comparative indifference of the infant or the animal (which is due entirely to the lack of differentiating equipment) but is due to an effort at desensitization and immobilization of the specifically human apparatus, resulting in paralysis and projection, impotence and paranoia.

III.

All Man's endeavor to facilitate the process of living appears to have led not to the genuine overcoming of suffering and the achievement of enjoyment in human creativeness, but only to a blunting of suffering and enjoyment alike, so that the human being is lingering in the limbo of "discontent within our civilization." At this point it seems to be most necessary to find a re-orientation toward the experience and evaluation of suffering. Contemporary Man is still burdened with Adam's concept of suffering as punishment, e.g., as retribution or deterrent. The guilt feeling, the feeling of sinfulness, is a complete withdrawal from the attempted act ("I should not have done it; I wish I hadn't done it; I shall never do it again! *Pater peccavi*."). But this withdrawal makes sense only if there is failure (fallibility); one does not regret success. It implies the expectation of immediate satisfaction, which would give Man the feeling of perfection and omnipotence. Primitive Man — like His Majesty the Baby — is impatient and greedy and unable to stand tension. As he is as yet unaware of what he eventually may become, he experiences the animal status quo as perfect and expects from every move he makes immediate restoration of this animal perfection.

Here is where the Devil comes in, the genius of the shortcut, the betrayer of God and Man with the promise of easy and immediate achievement (omnipotence = likeness to God).

It is not incidental that the serpent could become and remain the eternal image of the tempter, the deceiver, the Devil. The worm that, for a few moments at a time, achieves a nearly upright position, serves as a perfect symbol of homo sapiens at the earliest stage of his human development, pretending to be further and to know better than is actually true at any particular moment. It is the limited, "perfect" but deceptive, obsessional knowledge, based on the assumption of pretentious posture and the concoction of precocious interpretation, which is rejected by God as "not in His image." The pretentious skin must be shed again and again, revealing the original worm crawling away in the dust.

But God reveals Himself only as far as Adam can comprehend himself. "Of dust thou art and to dust thou shalt return." For Adam these are the only relevant characteristics of Man: his beginning as a worm and his end in death. But between dust and dust Man creates himself in the image of God, as much as is realizable at any given moment. Like any other obsessional neurotic, who imposes a prematurely conceived pattern on the whole of existence, Adam mistakes the partial for the total, the incidentals: Devil and Death, for the essential: God as He reveals Himself in Man.

Adam rejects the inexperienced and incomplete self-realization in the image of God. Having fallen out of the completeness of the animal instinct cycle, he feels guilty, e.g. cast out of his matrix and disoriented. He is unable to recognize and to realize the infinity of God in his own infinite potentialities. But Death and the Devil are always complete and finite; so for Adam and all his kin for hundreds of generations, Death and the Devil become pointers for orientation, perverted signposts with the help of which the misguided human fumbles his way through life. Condemned to ignorance, suffering and death, Adam and his progeny slave through the centuries while a merciless God, all-knowing and unsuffering, looks on.

IV.

A few thousand years later, God is no more a mere onlooker. He has come to earth as a simple working man, suffering poverty, torture and death. Wearing the thorny crown of Man's suffering, carrying the cross of Man's sinfulness, being forever nailed to it and dying on it, he is forever sharing in the suffering of humanity and by this act of participation, relieving Man's guilt feeling for his inadequacy, his imperfection, his unlikeness to God: *Ecce Homo.*

Since the time of Adam, this is the greatest and most incisive step in Western human development. It enables Man to save himself from the Fall, from the intolerable degradation of having become human (fallible). The condescension of God to the human level of error and suffering and death makes Man acceptable to himself.

But here another dichotomy creeps in. It seems that in the closer union of God and Man and in the mode of development that has been facilitated by Christianity, the Holy Ghost has gone to the Devil. The very agent that brought about Man's spiritual development — from the frightened ape that fell from the tree of Paradise, to the human being whose very suffering is in the image of God — the Holy Spirit of Creative Imagination has been abandoned in the process of Christianization. "There is a sense in which the creative imagination is repugnant to Christianity and to any fixed embodied myth."* By the choice of bread and wine — the earliest ingenious utilizations of natural resources that Man's creative imagination has devised to satisfy his most primitive needs — as symbols of Christ's suffering and sacrifice, Man has displaced the biological emphasis on creativeness onto a by-product of the creative process.

Of course, in the beginning of human development Man's creativeness seemed pitifully and eternally distant from any reflection of God's creative imagination. The more undifferentiated and undirected human creativeness is at any time, the greater is the suffering and dissatisfaction connected with it, and the greater is the need for a life hereafter, to make up for the frustrations and disappointments in this life on earth. But while Adam regards his suffering as a curse, as something that inherently divides him from God and shows him up in his inadequacy and fallibility, the Christian accepts his suffering as Man's foremost and noblest characteristic, as something that entitles him to a place on the right hand of God. By stabilizing something that is incidental to human development as final, as the essential and eternal and most desirable characteristic of Man, the Christian gives up the Holy Ghost, the spirit of creative development, and resigns

---

*Rayner Heppenstall: "Two Novels by Leon Bloy," *Partisan Review,* 1948.

himself to a devitalized existence of stagnation ("Blessed are the meek and mild," "Blessed are the poor in spirit.") and the hope of eternal happiness in the life hereafter.

V.

The first Biblical story of the Creation of the Universe contains a much more valid representation of the ever-present Creative Spirit than the Christian myth: "And the Spirit of God hovered over the waters." Nothing could symbolize more forcefully the state of "Creative Indifference," the zero-point from which every development is possible. And the myth of the seven-day process of the Creation of the World is still a valid symbolization of both, natural history and God's Creative Imagination, become world.

But the seventh day is long past, and God is not resting indefinitely. Man's creative imagination in shaping his own development is a logical continuation of the Creation of the Universe. Original Sin does not lie in Adam's inexperienced identification with God's Creative Imagination, but in his inexperienced alienation of it as evil, as originating in his association with the Devil, as leading only to suffering, frustration and death.

Of course, there is suffering and there is evil. Evil is whatever spoils the creative process, whatever blocks the process of integrated and integrating development. So certainly suffering based on repression and inhibition of vitality and creative imagination (the mainsprings of human development) must be evil, e.g., futile, dissipating, destructive, superfluous, what we now call neurotic. But there is another type of more genuine suffering, that is an inherent part of the creative process itself; the pangs of birth, the torment of the artist, the scientific doubts, which are characteristics of a vigorous process in its most dynamic stages. Once a definite valid gestalt has emerged (the child, the work of art, the mathematical formula), the tension is relieved (suffering is nothing else but unrelieved tension) and there is satisfaction and joy.

The Old Testament does not tell us anything about the suffering of God in creating the world; it needed a life and death of Christ to make up for this immature omission and to give suffering its rightful place in creative development. The creative process, of which Christ's Suffering is representative, is a revolutionary social and spiritual development from patriarchy to potential socialism, emphasizing the rights of the Mother and the Son beside the Father's, the carpenter's against the ruling priesthood's, the underdog's against the powers that be. But by elevating suffering to a state of value independent of the creative process that it is part of, Christianity opens the door to repression and inhibition and leads itself *ad absurdum*.

If the story of the world's creation does not betray God's suffering, it certainly shows God's joy and satisfaction in having completed a formative process: "And He saw that it was good." Adam in his apelike incompetence could not realize his God-likeness in the enjoyment of achievement; he was too involved in suffering in the formative process of becoming human. In the throes of the birth pangs the mother is only aware of pain, not of the child, just as, after the completion of the birth, she is only aware of the child and has forgotten the pain. These two essential aspects of the creative process are neatly separated in the Biblical story and assigned to different protagonists: God has all the fun, while Adam has all the pain. No wonder that, without the relief of achievement, he looks at creativeness with suspicion and distrust, and regards its indispensable suffering as a curse. Christianity tried to straighten out this distortion of the meaning of the creative process by raising the status of suffering from its neglected and despised position to divine rank. But its actual biological counterpart, the enjoyment and achievement aspect of the creative process, has only a secondary place in the Christian concept. The dead Christ is buried and a stone is placed on his tomb, so that his ascension after three days appears as a miraculous reward for his suffering rather than an intrinsic part of his creativeness. There probably originates the expectation of a life hereafter as a reward (heaven) or punishment (hell) for a life on earth. The Spanish Inquisition, saving lost souls by the imposition of torture and death by fire, is the logical Christian reaction to the creative humanist development of the Renaissance, which revived the ancient Greek approach, the excitement and curiosity aspect which stresses achievement and enjoyment and victory over adversity.

VI.

While Christian mythology is oriented predominantly on suffering, frustration, and death, and had to invent an afterlife — in heaven where you are rewarded for your earthly sufferings, or in hell where you are punished for ever and ever if you dared to enjoy yourself during your lifetime — ancient Greek mythology is mainly based on the achievement aspect and scotomizes to a great extent the doubts and sufferings of any developmental process. Athena springs forth from the head of Zeus painlessly and complete. The Greek ideal is the Hero, Man who is not deterred by difficulties and disappointments, but who overcomes them and achieves a position beyond and above them. The Hero is elevated, even during his lifetime, to the rank of the Gods (Theseus, Hercules, etc.).

But where is the place of Prometheus? Chained to the rock and having his liver picked by an eagle, he is Christ on the Cross carrying the burden of Man's suffering in the process of his human development. But Prometheus is also the instigator and promoter of this development, Lucifer, the light — and life-bringer. And he is also Adam, worried by his conscience and taking his suffering as punishment.

"Notes on the Mythology of Suffering and Sex" was written in 1949. This is its first publication in English.

5.

The Psychoanalyst and the Critic

Daniel E. Schneider's *The Psychoanalyst and the Artist* (Farrar, Straus, 1950) is a delightful and exasperating book. It is delightful in its wealth of pertinent material, in the observation, description and interpretation of often innumerable psychoanalytic, artistic and literary data; it is exasperating and disappointing in many of its theoretical premises and conclusions. The confusion is due partly to an indiscriminate use of Freudian terminology; partly to a sliding off (despite promises to the contrary) from the analysis of the work of art to the analysis of the artist; but mainly to a half-naive, half-"scientific" tendency to simplification, a disregard for the actual complexities and difficulties in the psychoanalytic as well as the artistic processes. As any reader will easily recognize the positive aspects of the book and will find a host of valuable information and stimulation, it may be more useful here to point out some of the most significant fallacies.

It seems to me rather naive to take *truth* and *beauty* as starting points for the discussion of the artistic process. We achieve, if we are lucky, truth and beauty as a point of arrival after a complicated and laborious voyage. The main concern of the artist is certainly not the "exercise of esthetic transformation" of truth into beauty, but the organization of a multitude of various, disparate, incompatible experiences — which threaten the individual or society with disintegration and therefore are experienced as ugly — into a meaningful, integrated whole, a unity within which they make sense and which therefore is or may be experienced as beautiful.

The measure of a great artist cannot possibly be, as Dr. Schneider thinks, the degree to which he promotes a process of identification in his audience. The effect of any mediocre popular film or sentimental song is precisely that it makes the process of identification so easy that any more differentiated organizing process becomes superfluous. Identification makes use of the infantile mechanisms of confluence (hanging on, swallowing whole), while integration needs the more developed processes of contact and assimilation (chewing through, digestion). Identification is easiest where the actual life or the ideal dream is simply mirrored, but not organized into a new, more meaningful unity. Therefore the majority of people identify more readily with Willy Loman than with Hamlet, with Grandma Moses than with Chagall, with the Chocolate Soldier than with Figaro.

It would be a sorry state of affairs indeed, if the clue to form was only "the knowledge of all the implications of identification." If this were true, it would only make for multiple identifications: an acute neurotic conflict, if simultaneous; an "as if" personality, if successive. The artistic creation is precisely the overcoming of these multiple identifications, and their integration (for the artist himself and for his audience) in a new self awareness. Any work that does not produce this new self-realization is not a work of art.

The emphasis on identification as the foremost creative agent leads itself *ad absurdum* in the attempt to explain the fact that some people are more "gifted" than others. Leaning heavily on Freud (*Leonardo da Vinci*), Dr. Schneider maintains that the particularly gifted child goes through a period of intense "sexual" curiosity and identifies not only with father and mother, but with the "unseen" act, the "unfelt" pleasure and the "unforeseen but inevitable" result of sexual creativity. This highly speculative explanation gets effectively around what I should consider as the crucial point, namely that "gifted" children identify not so much with mother or father or other authoritative images, as with their own processes of growing and developing and discovering the world. They are from the very beginning more truly "themselves," not just bundles of identification. They are also not paranoiacs who project their own creativeness on their objects of observation and have to repossess it by identification.

Thus, Freud's "narcissistic reservoir," the "neutral" source of energy (rather than the father-mother identification) is nothing else than the predominant self-awareness;

primary narcissism is not, as Dr. Schneider will have it, a negative thing, but the primary self-awareness of the child, the way he "is" and "has himself." It is this primary self-awareness and its development beyond and above the customary identifications that make the creative artist.

The schizophrenic, on the other hand, is the "secondary narcissist" whose love is retroflected onto himself because "otherness" to him is a threat and cannot possibly be lovable; not because he is aware of himself as the only lovable object, but because he is as unaware of himself as he is unaware of others.

Dr. Schneider defines the artistic gift as the gift for and the technique of transformation of our *dreams*. In my opinion, art is a way of transforming or, better, organizing *real* experience. Dreams are distorted and abortive attempts (Freud calls them acts of "inner dishonesty") to organize reality, a shunting-off of the forces that could lead to an increased self-realization onto a dead rail, where they will be forgotten. Only by way of interpretation — i.e., transformation of the unintelligible dream material into something more meaningful for the actual life situation — can these forces again be made available. But this does not necessarily and immediately mean a complete and satisfactory organization of experience; it means simply the discovery of raw material and the removal of blocks. It is psychoanalysis, not art.

In his endeavor to emphasize the similarities in the artistic and psychoanalytic processes, Dr. Schneider overlooks continually the essential difference, namely that the artist is himself the "dreamer," interpreter and transformer, and consequently the work of art is "dream," interpretation, and transformation all in one; while the psychoanalyst is at best a mediator (by interpretation) between the dream (neurotic conflict) and the transformation (the new self-realization, the cure) of the *patient*. In psychoanalysis the parts are divided, the analyst is not himself involved in the patient's conflict, his interpretation is an entirely conscious analytical procedure, and the final transformation in turn is again predominantly the experience of the patient. The artist, on the other hand, is completely involved; the pressure of the conflict urges the transformation, but the awareness of the conflict, its interpretation and transformation is all *one*; the conflict is admitted to full awareness only at the point where the means for its interpretation and transformation are available (otherwise there would be a neurotic breakdown). The interpretative, analytical aspect of the artist's work is the least conscious one, and always more obvious to the audience than to the artist himself, who very often is not (and need not be) aware of all the implications of his work. Why and how that is so is as much of a riddle after Dr. Schneider's painstaking efforts, as it has ever been before, and love's labor, alas, is lost again.

Dr. Schneider might have fared better if he had likened the psychoanalytic approach not to art, but to *criticism*. As the psychoanalyst is a mediator between dream and self-realization, so the critic is a mediator between dream and self-realization, so the critic is also a mediator a between work of art and its appreciation (resulting in a new self-realization) by its audience. His function is largely therapeutic; he tries to remove blocks to appreciation and to cure artistic insensitiveness. The respective critical methods are not in themselves good or bad, adequate or inadequate analytical approaches to a work of art, but either more or less applicable to different patients, spectators, readers, listeners, depending on their specific blocks, emotional, semantic, political, etc.

"In the United States at this time liberalism is not only the dominant but even the sole intellectual tradition." "The paradox is that liberalism is concerned with the emotions above all else, as proof of which the word happiness stands at the very center of its thought, but ... in the very interests of its great primal act of imagination by which it establishes its essence and existence — in the interests, that is, of its vision of a general enlargement and freedom and rational direction of human life — it drifts towards a denial of the emotions and the imagination." "It is one of the tendencies of liberalism to simplify ...so that when we come to look at liberalism in a critical spirit, we have to expect that there will be a discrepancy between what I have called the primal imagination of liberalism and its present particular manifestations." "The job of criticism would seem to be, then, to recall liberalism to its first essential imagination of variousness and possibility, which implies the awareness of complexity and difficulty."

These are quotations from Lionel Trilling's *The Liberal Imagination* (Viking Press, 1950), an important therapeutic attempt at mediation between the nearly forgotten liberal "dream" and a new liberal self-realization.

As is to be expected, Dr. Trilling does not make his most significant therapeutic contribution in the chapters on "Freud and Literature" or "Art and Neurosis." Yet his analysis of Freud illustrates a major diagnostic point made in an earlier chapter, namely that "a culture is not a flow, nor even a confluence; the form of its existence is struggle, or at least debate — it is nothing if not a dialectic. And in any culture there are likely to be certain artists who contain a large part of the dialectic within themselves, their meaning and power lying in their contradictions; they contain within themselves, it may be said, the very essence of the culture, and the sign of this is that they do not submit to serving the ends of any one ideological group or tendency." So Freud's deliberate, "scientific"- materialistic, nearly contemptuous approach to art as something akin to neurosis ("a substitute gratification," "an illusion in contrast to reality") in battle with his spontaneous insight into the constitution of the mind as a "poetry-making organ," results in a system with the quality of "grim poetry," a theory of man as "a creature of far more dignity and far more interest than the man which any other modern system has been able to conceive ... not to be understood by any simple formula (such as sex), but as an inextricable tangle of culture and biology."

These points in turn are amplified and rectified in the chapter on "Art and Neurosis." The "meaning and power" of the artist is of course not in the presence and representation of conflict, which would mean only suffering and possibly neurosis, but in the creative adjustment of the conflict, its "transformation" into something new, which is evidence par excellence of health and growth. Thus the artist (and the scientist) is not just the representative of the culture of his time, but by working out a new and (for his time) valid solution of the cultural-biological conflict, he becomes the leaven, the maker, the very essence of culture.

The merit of the attempt to save the spirit of Freud from his too-facile followers and critics (an act of grace which Freud himself performs most effectively for anyone who cares to read *him* and his style rather than most of his followers and critics) is much surpassed in liberal/therapeutic value by Dr. Trilling's analysis of a variety of literary and scientific material that is consumed (or rejected) by most educated Americans in the course of their liberal education. The different chapters group themselves easily into a pattern that illustrates most strikingly the cultural dialectic of our time: How certain books, originally written for grown-up readers, are now predominantly fit for adolescents and children, because of the inherent immaturity of their authors, e.g., Sherwood Anderson, the eternally spiteful adolescent, and Kipling, the eternal little boy who has to be "in" on the secrets of the grown-ups; as against, e.g., the importance of *Huckleberry Finn*, a book written for boys, but more and more appreciated by the adult mind, built not on the passing fancies of adolescence, but on the very fundamentals of human existence: the meaning of truth, the divinity of nature and human affection; or the *Immortality Ode*, "a poem about growing; not about growing old, but about growing up"; the general appreciation of Dreiser, "because his books have the awkwardness, the chaos, the heaviness which we associate with reality"; as against the rejection of James, whose very brilliancy and elegance is suspicious to the progressive liberal mind; the fallacies of the Kinsey Report, resulting from the purely quantitative approach to predominantly emotional problems ("There is something repulsive in the idea of men being studied for their own good." "Some paradox of our natures leads us, when once we have made our fellow men the objects of our enlightened interest, to go on to make them the objects of our pity, then of our wisdom, ultimately of our coercion"); as against the continued relevance of the moral-psychological imagination of Tacitus.

The remaining chapters are concerned not with the analysis of any particular work or author, but with ideas and attitudes, manners and morals, the ways and means of appreciation, and the cultural role of the novel as an art form. What emerges from the overwhelming flood of detailed observation, evaluation and indignation, *despite* a good many questionable statements, is a strong island of true liberalism, a good place for convalescence from the "progressive-scientific" epidemics of our adolescence. It offers ambulatory exercise with the help of a new liberal vocabulary that includes complication (as against simplification) historical sense (as against the slogan of "progressiveness"), diversity (as against uniformity), change (as against security and "stability") and humility — Mr. Trilling calls it "piety," the acceptance of the human condition, which is imperfection — as against the facile perfectionism of our fathers). An invigorating atmosphere, the "hum and buzz" of all the implications of liberal imagination, imparts a dynamic feeling of openness, not to be confused with "broad-mindedness," which is the further possible extension of an essentially narrow attitude, a dead end. *The Liberal Imagination* is a book "about growing; not about growing old, but about growing up."

One of the major points that Dr. Trilling makes abundantly clear is that the specialized training in contemporary techniques, which nowadays passes for education, is unable to produce the sensitive responsibility that is necessary and desirable for the continued existence of a true liberal democracy; it is certainly vastly inadequate to inspire competent "social therapists": scientists, educators, psychoanalysts, politicians, who can do justice to the varied and complex possibilities of their charges only if their own cultural background is wide and deep, if their special knowledge and technique is illumined by their own creative imagination in contact with the creative imagination of the centuries.

Under these optimal conditions, the psychoanalyst and the critic may indeed be likened to the artist. They, too, are on the side of the angels: mediators, conveyors of "meaning" between "heaven" and "earth" (the stages of greater and lesser integration), messengers flying on the wings of creative imagination, symbolized in more imaginative periods of history as Hermes, Pegasus, and the Dove.

"The Psychoanalyst and the Critic" originally appeared in Volume II (1950) of *Complex*, a magazine edited by Dr. Perls's friend and professional associate, Paul Goodman.

6.

Notes on the Psychology of Give and Take

"It's give and take." This most felicitous English phrase (no other language has its equal) indicates the very essence of relationship. "To give" and "to take" are not merely transitive verbs in the narrow grammatical sense. They imply as objects not only what is given or taken, but the act of giving and the act of taking, both having each other as objects. Between them they comprise the whole range of the social process, the aim of which is the balance of the social field, while growth continues.

The alert, ongoing, ever-changing awareness of the plus and minus in the social situation we call Justice. Justice is blind; for the eye — according to the figure-ground formation — is the organ of preference. The kinesthetic sense is the organ of balance, so Justice is pictured holding a pair of scales, and to balance them, "it's give and take."

Spontaneous Give and Take

A PRESENT is something that just "is," held out, offered.

The German word for a present is *"Geschenk."* *Schenken"* means "pouring out"; *"der Schenke"* is the man who pours wine at table (Songs of Hafiz, West-Oestl, Divan, etc.); *"die Schenke"* or *"der Ausschank"* means "the inn." *Geschenk* is thus something poured out, overflowing, obtained without effort. It comes from abundance (cornucopia, Mother Earth, Land of Milk and Honey, etc.).

A present is not a sacrifice, but something that is given easily and without expectations on the side of the giver. It is also not a surprise or reward, but what is naturally expected and looked for in an established community, as the baby expects the mother's milk. For the infant everything is (or should be) *Geschenk*, the natural, easy fulfillment of natural desire.

The infant is not (and need not be) grateful. Gratitude is the response to the unexpected gift, to the undeserved benefit, in short, to an act of grace. One feels grateful for the release from guilt feelings, for the re-establishment of the feeling of belonging. One does not feel and express special gratitude for what is coming to him in the natural course of events, within which it is as compelling for the mother to give as it is for the child to receive nourishment.

The present restores the integrity of the giver as well as of the receiver. The free correspondence between abundance and need guarantees the balance of the social field.

Christmas Old-Style

The original oral significance of the present is very obviously expressed in the European Christmas customs. Santa Claus comes with a big sack chock full of nuts, fruit, and candy which he empties in the middle of the room, and all the kids grab as much as they can hold. In Germany the *pièce de résistance* of every individual heap of Christmas presents is a plateful of the traditional Christmas cookies, nuts, raisins, fruit, candy, etc. Prior to the industrial manufacture of Christmas decorations, the main decorations of the Christmas tree, apart from candles, were edible. The tree, studded with lights and laden with food in the middle of winter, is a happy manifestation of man's sense of abundance and justice, symbolizing the effort to compensate for the darkness and barrenness of nature.

Presents were given mainly to children and other dependents, to the poor, etc.

The main event of Christmas Day was the big meal, the feeding of servants, employees, orphans, paupers, etc. Grown-ups in the same social or economic category did not give each other presents, as that would have meant imposing and incurring obligations, which would run contrary to the true spirit of *Schenken.* And certainly no dependent was expected to put himself to any expense for a present to anyone better off than himself, i.e., to make a sacrifice. The needy had a natural right to the present, without obligation, without "deserving," etc.

The same attitude is reflected in the custom of giving birthday presents. For your birthday you get something not because you are needy, let alone "deserving," but simply because you "are." With the recognition of your existence as a human being, your potential neediness is taken for granted. The world is a present for every human child; the good and bad fairies or the Three Wise Men are present at every birth. Adults, who all the year round deprive children of their birthright, atone by giving Christmas and birthday presents.

Christmas New-Style

Atonement is not an act of justice; it is not based on the acute and responsible awareness of actual need. It stems from the vague sense of obligation which, in the complicated structure of our society, is replacing more and more the spontaneous and discriminating awareness of relationship. Nowadays the Christmas or birthday present makes up not so much for the need of the receiver as for the guilt feelings of the giver. Thus, it does not restore the balance of the social field, but creates additional unbalance through disappointment on the side of the receiver and resentment on the side of the giver, who, in order to alleviate his guilt feelings and to produce a semblance of social balance, has to invest the Christmas gift with a significance far beyond its actual value. He becomes an advertising agent who has to convince the receiver that he really needs and wants what he is getting. As little as possible is spent on gifts that are made to look worth a million. "Good will to men" becomes something printed smaller and smaller on more and more artistic

Christmas cards and packed, in niggardly amounts and inferior quality, in more and more ingenious wrappings.

The sense of obligation is the vague acceptance of social involvement without the acute awareness that would make the discharge of obligation a limited and socially valid act. Discharge of obligation does not release giver and receiver into a more balanced relationship, but creates a new bond, as the name indicates, of unlimited mutual obligation. Thus, it introduces the whole vicious circle of competition and bribery, futile sacrifice, disappointment, resentment, and guilt. The annual Christmas farce leaves everybody exhausted physically, emotionally, financially; in January we are sick, mean, and broke. From a symbol of man's love and justice, Christmas has degenerated into a racket, the very characteristic of which is that it throws the social process out of balance.

As in our urbanized and industrialized civilization it has become increasingly difficult and in fact impossible to be fully aware of the social situation and one's place in it, many previously effective social attitudes (measures to restore balance in the social field) have become distorted and invalid.

Creative and Injurious Sacrifice

Making a SACRIFICE originally implied the giving up of something of lesser for something of greater value. It breaks up the wholeness of personal integrity in order to achieve integrity on a superpersonal level. As the word "sacrifice" indicates, it has mainly a religious (or social, which is originally the same) significance. It means making oneself whole through communion with the Divine; giving up the pleasures on earth for the life hereafter; sacrificing one's sexuality for the love of Christ or one's private life for the good of the community.

The sacrifice would place an enormous responsibility on the receiver, if it were not that in the religious or social context the sacrificer makes himself responsible (by prayer and meditation and social activity), so his sacrifice will not be in vain. He need not burden God or society with guilt feelings even for his nonachievement, for by his very sacrifice he is absolved from his own guilt feelings. Thus the sacrifice, however great, never amounts to a real deprivation, but to an intrapersonal restructuring of the personality, away from more personal and along more impersonal lines.

In interpersonal relationships, on the other hand, the sacrifice amounts practically to a bribe. A strong love or family relationship may be a borderline case (the sexual context, too, is impersonal), but any interpersonal contact tends to place all responsibility for the sacrifice of something lesser for something greater on the receiver. The sacrificer expects the receiver to grow on his sacrifice, i.e., to show and appreciate his (the receiver's) gain, which alone would make the sacrifice worthwhile. The impersonal sacrifice tries to elicit from the receiver something (love, affection, recognition, gratitude, etc.) that otherwise might not be forthcoming. The sacrificer lacks self-esteem and tries to force it from the receiver, i.e., he inflates whatever he is giving or doing, he "rubs it in," so that the receiver should not for a moment forget it. As he has projected his own unrealized need for wholeness on the receiver, the sacrificer can never do enough and can never get enough. He continually tries to escape his own guilt feelings by throwing them on the receiver.

While the genuine superpersonal sacrifice gives up something of definitely appreciated personal value for the union with something greater, the interpersonal sacrifice buys personal appreciation and thus compensates for the lack of self-esteem. Disappointment is inevitable, for the more that is given, the more that is taken for granted by the receiver, so that less and less appreciation is forthcoming, while the sacrificer gets progressively more and more impoverished and disintegrated.

While the interpersonal sacrifice is usually made by immature and insecure people, the genuine (superpersonal) sacrifice is an act of maturity and insight. The Buddha gives up a life of pleasure and dissipation for the way of poverty and concentration at the age of forty. Christ walks to the Cross at the age of thirty-three. Abraham prepares to sacrifice Isaac, whom he has begotten in his old age, and only at the last moment is he blessed by the insight that his own personal sacrifice of the apple of his eye is as nothing compared with the promise of future generations upon generations living in the sight of the Lord. To resign the sacrifice, and with it one's own immediate intrapersonal integration, is perhaps the greatest sacrifice — so great, indeed, that Abraham in his senility (or childishness) is not quite able to carry it off. The slaughtering of the ram in place of the original sacrifice again amounts to a bribe. It is a childish dummy device, a substitute that makes it possible to externalize one's guilt feelings (the evidence of lack of integration) and thus efficiently to prevent any intrapersonal or intra-group reorganization. The difference between the scapegoat and the golden calf is, after all, not so very great!

Bribery and Blackmail

The BRIBE is an *a priori* payment for a not yet committed betrayal. In order to be successful, the bribe has to be attractive enough, i.e., of sufficient material or social advantage to the receiver, to tempt him to make a switch in moral allegiance. It must be strong enough to break a previous commitment and to overcome the guilt feelings connected with such a break by forming a more promising bond of loyalty.

Only the dissatisfied and frustrated are open to bribery; only the greedy and insatiable are prone to pay bribes. It is, in fact, the same type of person who, depending on actual circumstances, either pays or takes bribes. It is the infantile, insecure hanger-on, who does not feel convinced of the legitimacy of his own needs and demands and who has no confidence in his ability to command consideration and respect.

Both the giver and receiver of a bribe are open to BLACKMAIL and are potential blackmailers. They have to take good care of each other: the briber's generosity must never flag; the bribed one's subservience must be perpetually assured. As the briber and the bribed feel equally guilty, they feel equally threatened by exposure. And blackmail is nothing else but extortion (of money or other advantages) by the threat of exposure.

Of course, bribery is not an indispensable condition for blackmail. Indeed, any knowledge about anything that could potentially discredit anyone in the eyes of anyone else can be used for the purpose of extortion. Where, as in a totalitarian society, the disintegration of individual human relationships becomes a political goal, bribery and blackmail become the foremost political devices.

But we have learned from experience in our own time that no balanced society can be established by methods that are liable to increase the guilt feelings and to produce the mutual contempt of its members. The degree of callousness and brazenness necessary to get rid of the ensuing depression sets in motion the whole para-noiac process of desensitization and projection, suspicion, feeling attacked and persecuted, looking for scapegoats, attack and destruction, and finally self-destruction.

Payment and Reward

One should expect that the most successful way of balancing the social process would be an exact exchange of values. But unfortunately, "an eye for an eye and a tooth for a tooth" applies only in the field of retribution and punishment. Since it first was refuted by the Wisdom of Solomon, much ink has flowed already to prove the invalidity of this primitive principle, which presupposes an undeveloped, undifferentiated sense of values, i.e., an unawareness of the necessities and possibilities in the actual situation.

We shall confine ourselves here to a discussion of two other aspects of value exchange, namely, PAYMENT and REWARD.

Payment is made as a monetary or material equivalent either for goods or for work. It is given in recognition of value, which in turn is defined by temporary economic circumstances, depending on supply and demand.

Reward, on the other hand, is an expression of appreciation of merit. Any meritorious action stands alone, "on its own merit." There are no comparable standards of value that could be adequately expressed in money. Thus, a reward may consist of a sum of money (which then is quite arbitrarily decided on), but it may also consist of a medal or a diploma or a title, or the recognition and gratitude of one's fellowmen, or simply in the consciousness of a thing well done.

Promotion in military or civil service is partly a reward, an appreciation of merit. But as far as it is expected with regularity and connected with continuing material advantages it is payment for service.

The American or European physician is paid for services rendered on a generally accepted scale, so and so much per visit or operation or psychotherapeutic session. The Chinese physician is paid when his cure has been successful, i.e., he is rewarded for a unique effort.

In a general way one could say that the more meritorious the effort, i.e., the more it contributes to a genuine social balance, the less it is rewardable in money. Thus, the police reward, which is promised and given for information, is simply payment for betrayal, which falls more under the category of "bribery" than "reward." On the other hand, "virtue is its own reward." The most incessant and selfless services and sacrifices remain not only unpaid and unrewarded, but must be taken for granted. Only the limited work or object can be paid for with a limited amount of money; only the limited service or effort can be rewarded with promotion or a title or a citation. The unlimited devotion of a parent or the lifelong dedication to a cause cannot be paid for or rewarded; it can only be accepted and need not even be recognized. Its reward is in the actual performance, in the feeling of restoring the social balance in a changing ongoing process.

"Notes on the Psychology of Give and Take" originally appeared in Volume IX (1953) of *Complex*, a magazine edited by Dr. Perls's friend and professional associate, Paul Goodman.

7.

Notes on Fundamental Support of the Contact Process

When I announced last term that I intended to have a workshop on contact and support functions, someone made the remark that I would have to be very careful not to re-introduce a split into the holistic concept of the functioning of the organism. Well, I don't think that the assumption of support and contact functions constitutes a dichotomy, but rather a differentiation according to the figure/ground principle.

Support and contact are not separate problems on the purely instinctual level; at a more primitive stage of biological development, there is more confluence. Stages of development span over the worm, four-footer, ape to man with his developed cortex and upright posture where step by step the state of pure confluence withdraws.

All who have had some experience of Gestalt therapy, either as students or as patients, are familiar with the concept of contact. Contact is the recognition of "otherness," the awareness of difference. It is the boundary experience of "I and the other." I would differentiate between "being in contact" and "making contact." *Being in contact* indicates a continuing state which gradually tends toward indifference (confluence). *Making contact is a foreground* function, alert, awake, etc.

It requires a specific awareness of contact, e.g., of a specific object, activity, etc. For this reason, orientation and manipulation happen by way of a specific organ or specifically structured activity. At the same time, constitutional factors, primary physiology, posture as well as acquired habits which become automatic and thus equivalent to primary physiology, play a decisive role. Support for making contact comes from what has been assimilated and integrated.

The rest of the organism is *background* function, normally unawares, taken for granted, but indispensable *support* for the foreground function of contact.

February 16, 1953

Contact and support does not equal Conscious and Unconscious. The Unconscious, as far as it is the repressed or the introjected, is not support, but the very lack of it, interference, blockage; whereas support stems from an uninhibited primary physiology including assimilated and integrated experience. The most essential function for support is breathing. A mobile diaphragm is an absolute necessity for uninhibited breathing. Breathing is for life itself more important than drinking, eating and digesting. The acute awareness of discrepancy between support and contact functions is experienced as anxiety. Lack of oxygen as a prototype of anxiety is, at the same time, experienced as lack of essential support altogether. Normally, breathing is involuntary, happening automatically. In Gestalt therapy we are concerned with the disturbance and interruptions of this automatic process. I prefer to focus my attention here on the habitual interruptions of support functions excluding constitutional deficiencies and organic illness as well as lack of social support.

March 16, 1953

Therefore, today we shall concentrate on support methods and attitudes which are not characteristic for the whole human species (like upright posture and breathing, or the differentiation of manipulation into right and left-sided activity). We are going to talk about attitudes of making contact, which are specifically acquired either by individual people or by groups, nations, social classes, etc. Through repetition and formalization these contact functions become automatic, e.g., they become support functions if they facilitate, or resistance functions (support to noncontact) if they block the desired or necessary contact.

We speak about HABITS when we mean *personal behavior patterns* and CUSTOMS when we refer to *social behavior patterns*. Customs are more or less binding, perhaps more (or at least for a longer duration) if they are laid down, say, in a code of law or a definite church ritual, but not much less (even for shorter periods of time) if formalized and enforced by education, social-economic, or political pressure.

Before we go on with the discussion of manners and mannerisms, let me say a few words about style.

STYLE *is a unique mode of making contact, based on the support of completely assimilated and integrated behavior patterns.* Style can be attributed to groups and classes, art movements and historical periods. But it can also be intensely personal, a unique individual development.

A person who has style — or to the extent that he has got style — does not come into therapy. One could rather say that the *purpose of therapy is to establish and develop style*, e.g., an integrated and integrating way of expression and execution (Weber!).

Therapy, therefore, is concerned with behavior patterns which for some reasons cannot be fully integrated into the background of a person or a group. For obvious reasons, we can't do very much about the law or the church, but in therapy we have to work on those attitudes which have become an unwritten social and personal code of behavior: habits, manners and mannerisms.

The boundaries between manners and mannerisms are fleeting. MANNERS are generally accepted personal habits which are meant to facilitate contact. More often than not they are acquired by introjection, i.e., without full awareness of their meaning and purpose. MANNER-ISMS, on the other hand, are originally conscious, attention-getting devices which, in their automatization seem to be exaggerated and out of proportion to the contact that they are supposed to support (fairy tale voice, histrionic gestures, little finger!).

Nevertheless, manners and mannerisms can and do become part of the style of a person or group, if they can be integrated into the personal or social or national background, e.g., if they support the desired contact. For the maintenance of a feudalistic society, for instance, the differentiation, according to class distinction, of social manners, fashions, use of language or location, etc., provides very adequate support. The strict etiquette, if adhered to by all concerned, prevents social friction. What it does to the individual is another matter.

But, even under the strictest class limitations, a high degree of expression and integration is possible, as we can see, i.e.,, in the art and literature and music of these periods.

Strict social formalism combined with the ritual of the church procedures, for instance, produces a musical style that culminates in BACH. But Bach, more than his predecessors and contemporaries, achieves a unique personal style, for which the cultural background provides only the framework.

The musical style that culminates in MOZART has as support the European court etiquette with its intricate manners and even mannerisms, which are also reflected in the visual arts, the fashions, the architecture, the interior decoration of the period. BEETHOVEN's style, on the other hand, can be understood only against the background of the French Revolution, with the breaking up of strict form and the abolition of rococo manners and mannerisms.

All together, one could say that the excess of mannerisms over serious concern is always an indication of decline of a period or of a person (Rococo!).

March 23, 1953

Language and Speech

Next to upright posture and manipulative development, LANGUAGE is a foremost human characteristic. It is an organ of expression and communication, of interpersonal and intercultural contact. Language has time-binding properties: contact with past and future.

Language acquired by every human being becomes part of support apparatus. So does speech, but there is one very important difference: Speech may be impaired or prevented by vocal or muscular or neural dysfunctions (deaf-mutes, paraplegics, laryngitis, etc.), without changing basically the characteristic human structure. COMPENSATION will set in immediately (sign language, writing, acting out, etc.). Thinking and reasoning processes remain intact, even if not conveyable. There is no immediate compensation for destruction of the language center. A long process of retraining and developing other centers is required. Injuries in this area result in reduction, not only of language, but of the world which is contacted and comprehended and even created through language (see Goldstein on brain injuries).

My interest here is not concerned with organic disturbances, but with language habits, which develop as support for contact, or as inhibitions and blocks.

1) *Language* in general: There are general characteristics of language such as audible or visible use of signs or words in an order in which they represent and communicate an experience or event.

2) *Mother tongue*. Safety factor in sameness of general language structure. Contact with people of different language is difficult or impossible, with helplessness and anxiety a response which often leads to hostility.

3) *Dialect*: The lack of command of dialect results in embarrassment and hostility leading to anxiety.

4) *Written* and *colloquial* language: Written language traditionally is more or less fixed; colloquial more dynamic and continually changing. My assumption is that written language offers support whereas colloquial language more contact function. Slang presents a partial counter-indication. It is a new, spontaneous, interesting way of making language contact either with known or new facts. As a support function (fashion, brazenness, etc.) it often becomes boring or inadequate, finally discarded for some new slang expression. If adequate, it becomes integrated into the whole traditional body of language and part of the general support apparatus.

We now come to certain uses of language, which fall under the heading of manners; they are general property, but they become individual automatic habits.

For instance: *proverbs* or *quotations* from the Bible or from poetry are originally most valid formulations of contact experiences and ideas; but if they become clichés, they are very questionable support. ("Honesty is the best policy!" cliché blots out awareness, thus honesty very often becomes tactlessness.)

Individual language difficulties are associated with three structural aspects: Vocabulary, spelling, and grammar.

Vocabulary: preferences and taboos: fashionable slang or scientific jargon and sex vernacular, "unmentionables," "the queen of Spain has no legs." Pseudo-preference: swear words, etc.

Spelling: simplifications and abbreviations, secret code; schiz letter: no now, know. Representative of sound and history.

Grammar: Sentence structure most important ingredient in national and personal language manners and style (see French and American!). A preference for *nouns* indicates labeling, *verbs* indicates greater active involvement.

There is an Ego language and an Id language. Usually there is more contact with the use of "I". "I am hungry" vs. "There is an emptiness in my stomach."

The use of "I" may be neutralized by *indirect* language: I think, I guess, I wonder, I would say, etc. Further removal from the person would be expressions like: It seems to me," "it appears as if," etc. Extreme forms are: "I guess I should say that it seems to me that there is an emptiness in my stomach."

The use of "I" is circumvented by "one," "you," "everybody," etc. The tendency for generalization avoids individual responsibility. Language and speech are the main social contact functions, whereby there is a double contact: I-you, I-it.

I ———— You

|

I ———— It

The best support is ensured by a technique which integrates these two-directional tensions according to the figure/ground principle. The more important contact becomes figural:

I/you: verbs and adverbs. They are more expressive, dynamic.
I/it: nouns (labels) and adjectives.

These differences may be illustrated by comparing the language of love and that of mathematical lecture:
The language of love: I — you; We: subjective
Scientific language: objective
Ordinary colloquial: a mixture; I speak with someone about something.

"Notes on Fundamental Support" was originally prepared for presentation to the New York Institute for Gestalt Therapy in 1953. It appears here in English for the first time.

8.

Two Instances of Gestalt Therapy

The two cases selected for presentation represent "typical" examples of a well-known clinical picture. Both patients come to therapy with similar complaints, namely, they have difficulties in contact and concentration. They are intelligent and gifted but second best. They cannot make adequate use of opportunities but think afterwards of what they could or should have said or done. They find it nearly impossible to start anything new and waste a lot of time and energy on repetitive "dummy" activities. Both are self conscious, feel awkward and ridiculous, think that most people don't care for them. Their concept of what they should be like amounts essentially to the ideal image of a near-Victorian lady or gentleman. Their main support is their pride in the ability to do without. Nevertheless, there is in both an all-pervading feeling of frustration and dissatisfaction. In short, the diagnostic emphasis in both cases would be on the obsessional and more-or-less paranoid character features.

However, the similarity in diagnosis does not necessarily indicate a similarity in therapeutic procedure. I have chosen two cases for this discussion, rather than a single one in order to demonstrate in greater detail the difference in therapeutic techniques which is necessary and possible by taking into account the uniqueness of the patient's contact (or avoidance) techniques and the availability (or lack) of support functions.

The assumption of contact and support functions does not, as it may appear at first glance, re-introduce a dichotomy into the holistic concept of the functioning of the organism but is a differentiation according to the figure/ground principle. Contact — the recognition of "otherness," the awareness of difference, the boundary experience of "I and the other" — is more-or-less alert, specific, concernful awareness and activity. It is so much "figure" in the organismic functioning that neurosis has been defined as *avoidance of contact*, and the different types of neurosis as different *stages of withdrawal* from, or limitation of, contact.

But "who is all eyes does not see." The contact functions, by way of a specific organ or a specifically structured activity, take place against a background of organismic functions which are normally unaware and taken for granted; yet these latter provide the indispensable support for the foreground function of contact. They comprise hereditary and constitutional factors (primary physiology, etc.); acquired habits which have become automatic and thus equivalent to primary physiology (posture, language, manners, techniques, etc.); and fully assimilated experience of any sort. Only what is completely assimilated and integrated into the total functioning of the organism can become support.

Thus contact and support are not identical with Conscious and Unconscious. The Unconscious, as far as it is the repressed and introjected, is not support but the very lack of it. It is interference with, and blockage of, successful contact.

If we redefine neurosis as a state of malcoordination of contact and support functions, and the different neuroses as different types of malcoordination, we may define the goal of therapy as the achievement of optimal coordination of contact and support functions. We also may in time, with further research, arrive at the realization of a functional typology of neurosis.

At this point I find the contact/support concept a useful tool in the therapeutic situation. It immediately takes into account the patient's total behavior, not only his history and his verbalizations. The patient learns to work with material that is immediately available to him in the actual situation, without speculation or interpretation, by taking stock of all the aspects of his actual behavior, by bringing into the foreground and making figure out of what usually remains unrealized in the background. The questions "How?", "What?", "Where?", or "What does this do for you right now?" take preference over "Why?" or "What for?"; description prevails over explanation, experience and experiment over interpretation. Working strictly from the surface, e.g., from the actual awareness at any given moment, we avoid the mistake of contacting depth material prematurely, that in the first place was and had to be "repressed" because at a certain point in the patient's history it was unsupportable. Making it available by interpretation of dreams or symbolic actions does not mean making it more usable but often causes a strengthening of the defense mechanisms, waste of time, or worse, loss of the material by projection. The "negative therapeutic reaction," like the negative reaction to any other experience, is the result of unsupported contact.

On the other hand, the strengthening and expansion of the support functions mobilizes the alienated emotions and potentialities for contact and makes formerly repressed depth material easily accessible. The process could be compared with the creation of a work of art (the highest form of integrated and integrating human experience) in which the conflict between a multitude of incompatible and unmanageable experiences is realized only at the point where the means for its interpretation and transformation become available.[*]

How the concepts of contact and support are applied in therapy will become more evident in the actual case discussions.

Case of Claudia

Claudia, a 25-year-old Negro girl, comes from a lower middle class West Indian background. The family is socially ambitious in a Victorian way; they try to emu-

---

[*]Laura Perls, "The Psychoanalyst and the Critic," *Complex 2*, 1950

late white society and to segregate themselves from "black trash" by strictness of morals and manners which in actual white society do not apply anymore. They are religious in an obsessional-conventional way.

Her father was domineering and rather brutal; he left the family when Claudia was about 12 to follow Father Divine. She has no contact with him now. Once terrified of him, she now feels only contempt. Her mother is meek and submissive, self-sacrificing, religiously moralizing. Her younger sister is pretty, feminine, soft, motherly-protective. A younger brother committed suicide while in jail, for an alleged and likely homosexual involvement.

The patient regards herself as emancipated. She is very intelligent, has a degree in social science, is a case-worker with a city agency. She is coffee-colored, tall and slim, quite attractive but indifferently dressed and made up. She is well-behaved, uses "refined" language, is princi-pled as to "what a young lady can or cannot do." Motori-cally, she is rather jerky; her voice has a hard edge to it. She is bony and rather flat-chested, her head thrown aggressively forward, the muscles in her broad, boyish neck tense. She is living at home with mother, sister, and aunts whom she scares and bullies, and a righteous, religious uncle whom she despises and is afraid of.

She comes for therapy because she is "just not good enough at anything." She is not interested enough in her work; she is afraid of, and feels contempt for her clients. She gets behind in her casework. She cannot concentrate on her studies and had to repeat several exams. Socially, she is awkward and unhappy. People don't like her; they seem to be scared of her. She cannot get hold of the "right" people; she cannot be alone, either. She diagnoses herself as paranoid and is afraid of insanity. Occasional suicidal fantasies are reported which she, herself, does not take very seriously. More serious are headaches which bother her, at times, for a period of several days. She complains that she can't wear feminine clothes and that she dreads going to dances and parties looking silly in frilly dresses. Nevertheless she goes, suffering agonies. The patient has no manifest sex life, feels vaguely excited by and vaguely attracted to both sexes. She condemns both inclinations, feeling wanton and sinful with the one, weird and perverted with the other.

She is also subject to numbers of obsessional rituals and habits, amongst them a severe hand-washing compulsion which she does not even mention. As these habits are her safety devices, her support attitudes, they are automatic and taken for granted. In spite of the emphasis on how sick, weak and confused she feels, and how she suffers, the patient gives the impression of competence, articulateness, and great strength.

The patient was seen once a week for three separate periods of seven to eight months since 1949. Interruptions were caused partially through time and money reasons but more through her inability to restart after long vacations or even after a week's interval. From 1952-3, after she had achieved a certain level of functioning, I did not see her until she returned, voluntarily, at the end of '53, to work through some difficulties that she had become aware of in the meantime. Since then, she has been working steadily, more and more concentrated and successfully, and is rapidly approaching the end of her treatment.

But we shall go back to the beginning. Her first sentence, after she had plunked herself down at the couch was, "I am in a bad way, doctor. You'll have to do something for me. I doubt if you can. You won't be any better than Dr. X. (a psychiatrist with whom she had worked for a short period and who had sent her to me). She couldn't do anything with me, etc., etc."

It was obvious that the patient was challenging and taunting me. She was making demands, telling me how to handle her, trying to dominate and control the situation. Of course, from her family history it became quite evident that she identified with the bullying father and tried to manipulate me into the role of the submissive, hardworking, despised mother. But during the first few minutes of the first interview I did not have this information and I did not need it. I had only to consult my own reactions to the patient's behavior, my awareness of being belittled and imposed upon, the feeling of hostility that she provoked in me, to realize the specific pattern that the patient was acting out in this meeting as well as in any other contact situation. For her it was a contest in which she had to get the better, a question of victory or defeat, nearly of life or death. When she is unable to control the situation, she gets confused and anxious and has to withdraw.

If I had allowed her to ramble on in the same vein, she would have felt only that she was getting away with it again, e.g., it would have increased and fortified her

contempt for the feminine sex and with it her own basic
inferiority feeling. If I had pointed out that she was
telling me my business, but that I was the doctor and
conducting therapy, I would only have provoked a sharp-
ened contest, as she would have been quite unable to
cope with the ensuing confusion. In fact, whenever she
felt that I was in some way getting the better of her, she
ran back to her former analyst and usually succeeded in
manipulating her either into accepting her for a visit or
at least an hour-long telephone conversation to gain
reassurance of her own superiority. Thus, in the first few
weeks of working with me, she went back frequently and
without telling me about it. At later stages, she went
sporadically and told me in the next session, at first
brazenly, "I went to see Dr. X... so what do you have to
say to that!," later on more and more embarrassed,
"(smile) you know, (wriggle) I called Dr. X. (blush)!"

In the first session, neither withdrawing from, nor
entering into, the contest pattern that the patient tried to
impose on the situation, I asked her if she really wanted
help. "Yes, of course, that's what I am coming for." I
pointed out that she was asking for help in a rather
peculiar fashion, not really asking for something that
under the circumstances she might reasonably expect but
demanding it as if I were trying to withhold something
from her and she had to assert her right to get it, "You
better, or else!" She did not really know me, yet she tried
to pigeonhole me, put a label on me from her store of
past experience and to fantasize what I was or was not
going to do in the future. The only thing that she did
not do was to consider me here and now (face to face), to

look and listen to me, to make contact with me and find out about me in the present actual situation. For a moment, the wind was taken out of her sails; she was deprived of her habitual support. She got a little confused and embarrassed, but quickly collected herself, threw her head forward and barked, "I don't know anything about your qualifications. Do you have any? For all I know you may be a quack!" I satisfied her curiosity in this respect, but then pointed out that again she had looked for reassurance from the past (this time *my* previous experience and training) rather than through an evaluation of whatever she could experience of me and through me in the present.

The following weeks and months were spent mainly in concentrating on the "here and now" experience. The patient was discouraged from dwelling too much on her history and family background. It soon became more and more evident to her that she used the past as a convenient excuse and justification and that she burdened the family with the whole responsibility for whatever she was now, so that she need not make any effort toward any relevant change now, in the present. The questions, "What effort?" or "Effort against what?" mobilized intensive work on her so-called laziness and lack of concentration and contact. It was pointed out that contact can be made easily and adequately only when support is adequate and continuous. The obvious *discontinuities* in her behavior, her jerky motions, the break in her voice, her shallow arhythmical breathing, her separation of head (mind) and body (animal), her double moral standards, her masculine-superiority fantasy against the reality of her

femininity — to name only a few — all were in turn
brought into the foreground to that degree of awareness
where — if not an immediate change, at least an experimental approach, a fantasy or homoeopathic play with
different modes of behavior — became possible.

The inability to concentrate for any amount of
time provided the first opportunity to make her aware in
more and more detail of her techniques of self-sabotage.
She came to therapy apparently with great interest in
helping herself, but in every session got very soon either
bored and somewhat foggy, erratic and distracted by
incidentals. She said, "I can make some sort of a start,"
(her head pushed forward, her voice raised, her eyes
piercing), "but then ..." (the head drooped, she looked
squashed, the voice fizzled out, the sentence remained
unfinished). A whole series of experiments was conducted around every detail of this "half-experience." She
learned to pay attention to the sound of her voice and
how she produced it. The voice did not carry through as
she gave herself no chance to re-inhale during the act of
speaking. The rhythm of breathing became arrested, the
diaphragm got fixed at the bottom of the exhalation, and
the voice had to be pushed out from the throat with great
tension in neck, face, and throat muscles. She found that
her speech was not really an expression, it did not come
from the center (e.g., from balanced posture and a continuity of rhythmical breathing, the indispensable support
for optimal functioning), but it was a "pre-tense" in the
literal sense of the word (coming from head and neck
only). Listening to her voice, she recognized spontaneously, with a shock, "I sound like my father, raucous,

bullying." Then, without pushing from the top, "And I shut up like my mother, confused, stupid." Her breathing became deeper, more rhythmical, she felt her "stomach getting warm. Now it is fluttering and twitching." And she started to cry. Thus, from the increasing self-awareness in the actual therapeutic situation, without digging into memories and without interpretation, the patient realized the double identification with both parents and the resulting inner conflict together with the means of resolving it.

Her motoric awkwardness and jerkiness also were revealed as part and parcel of the masculine pretense. Just as in conversation and argument only the head and voice came forward, so in actual motion in any direction or toward any object only the extremities moved, or rather jerked, while the torso remained rigid and the center of gravity (the pelvic region) was retracted. The joints were tight; there was no spring action and no swing in her movements. As she is tall and lanky, she looked and felt not just awkward, but grotesque. With increasing awareness and with the help of detailed exercises she acquired gradually more and more mobility, more continuity in breathing, more fluidity in motion. She felt "more energy, more confidence, more swing, more stride, more excitement." She started to play tennis and soon became quite proficient. She worked more easily and with greater interest, and she made new social contacts.

At this stage, she went through an intense homosexual phase. She still maintained a predominantly negative concept of femininity, together with a comparative rigidity and insensitiveness of the pelvic region.

During the last few months — after we had worked
through her initial disgust barrier (which in turn led to
some work on her eating and learning habits, her indiscriminate stuffing and gobbling and swallowing of food as
well as of information and principles and her feeling "fed
up") — she has developed more and more sensitiveness
and flexibility in her middle region and with it a greater
acceptance of herself and her possibilities as a woman.
She has become interested in and excited by men and has
lately had some intimate heterosexual experiences. She
does not feel too confident, yet, and it will take her some
time to develop more positive feminine "techniques."

Her former brazenness, the pretense of strength
which is not centrally supported, has given way to genuine
embarrassment, the awareness of a temporary malcoordination of contact and support functions, which means
uncertainty, curiosity mixed with reluctance, a little anxiety, and a lot of excitement. The patient's physical ap-
pearance has changed considerably, quite apart from the
changes in posture and coordination. Her bone structure, of course, is the same, but her bust is more developed, her thighs are heavier, her face is more relaxed and
looks rounder. Her menstrual period, which was usually
early (23 days), had become at first retarded (33-35 days),
and now more normal (28-30 days). She has found her
own style in clothes, which is feminine in a sporty way,
without frills, quite smart. She has, at least for the time
being, given up her job as a social worker and taken up
library work. She feels it gives her more support, in the
process of learning to handle herself with her own problems, than did her previous effort to manipulate other

people with their difficulties. She has left the home of her family and moved into a boardinghouse near the place where she is working. She is now considering sharing an apartment with a friend. Claudia has become in fact what formerly she only imagined, but in some way always wanted to be, an emancipated female.

Case of Walter

Walter, a 47-year-old male, is a Central European Jewish refugee. He comes from an impoverished middle–class family, which, nevertheless, provided him with a university education. He became a lawyer, but with his degrees invalid in the successive countries of his emigration, he had to enter business life. His father was an unsuccessful businessman, colorless, meek and mild, with no initiative. His mother was ambitious and domineering, bitter about the father's failure. She was irritable, inconsistent in her demands, more amiable when the son finally achieved some professional and social status. She died in an asylum, after a complete paranoiac breakdown in the emigration. A younger brother is happy-go-lucky, apparently unaffected by the family situation.

The patient is married to an intelligent, subtly manipulative woman. They have two children, one of whom is slightly spastic. He is fond of the children, but feels he does not handle them well; he is too anxious, too constraining. The originally quietly companionable marriage has lately become somewhat precarious. His wife, interested in psychology by way of the child's handicap and therapy, is undergoing therapy herself and becoming increasingly dissatisfied with their relationship, mainly with his indifference to her interests.

The patient looks tired, resigned, and old. He walks with a slight stoop, elbows tight to his body, feet shuffling. His expression is intelligent, but worried. The eyes dart furtively around looking for an "out," the mouth is set in an apologetic smile. His speech is hesitant, he talks only "when he is spoken to." The voice is monotonous, has a wailing quality.

He is dissatisfied and in a dull way unhappy with nearly everything in his life. He is not so much complaining as berating himself for being such a failure in business, in social contact, in family life. He postpones everything that is not strictly routine, minor business phone calls as well as major decisions. He dreads meeting people, has to break his head for something to say, feels awkward and self-conscious. He is afraid of losing old business connections and convinced of his inability to make new ones. In spite of all these obvious limitations and self-recriminations, the patient is not unsuccessful in business, makes a comfortable living as an agent for some foreign business concerns, has kept the same accounts for many years, and is appreciated for his reliability and foresight. His children love him. He also has a small number of good friends. He gets great enjoyment from being out in the open, in contact with nature. But this more positive information was not available at the beginning of his therapy.

The patient was seen twice weekly for about four months (March through June 1953), then once weekly with an additional weekly group session, for ten months.

Group therapy proved particularly effective in this case, and the patient is still a member of a therapy group, while his individual treatment has been terminated.

In his first interview the patient stumbled into the room not looking right or left, as if he were wearing blinkers. He sat down at the edge of a chair, literally "on edge," squirming, saying nothing for several minutes. To my question, "What brings you here?" he clasped his arms tightly, shrugged his shoulders, finally mumbled diffidently, with a faint undertone of irritation and nagging, "I don't know what I am coming for ... my wife thinks I should ... I don't think it is of any use ... I don't know what to say ... my wife says ... " etc., etc. (shrug, collapse).

I felt somewhat squashed, too, and a little bored. The patient had, at least for the moment, achieved his neurotic aim: he put me off, he bored me with his monotonous wail and his repetitiousness, in fact, he did his best to discourage me from becoming interested. Obviously he regarded the whole situation as a nuisance and wanted to be left alone. But in presenting this entirely negative front he also exposed in detail the techniques which supported his withdrawal pattern and thus, quite unintentionally, provided me exactly with what he so desperately tried to withhold, the very "handle" by which he could be reached.

Again, as in the previous case of Claudia, it was pointed out to the patient that his way of asking for assistance was not too well designed for actually obtaining it, but, if anything, watered down whatever interest one might develop in doing anything for him. "Yes," his voice sounded much stronger now, nearly defiant, "I know I am boring. I never know what to say. I don't like asking people for anything. I always worry what they expect of me. I have to figure out what I should say; it takes too much time and I know only afterwards what I should have said."

Considering the question how all this applied in the actual therapy situation, the patient discovered that he was always so busy anticipating other people's needs and demands or berating himself for having missed out on something in the past, that he had no chance to realize his own needs and interests and actions in any present situation, even when it was specially designed for no other purpose but his own self-realization.

It took a number of months to make him realize that what he felt was not, as he maintained, "nothing," but rather discomfort, tension, impatience, irritability, distrust, apprehension; that what he did also was not "nothing," but rather pulling himself together, suspending animation, waiting for something to be over which might be a business meeting, an argument with his wife, or a therapy session.

Listening to his voice, the patient found to his surprise not only that he sounded like his father (a fact that he had always known) but also, particularly when he was berating and belittling himself, that he sounded like his mother having an argument with his father. The suspended-animation attitude thus was revealed as a most adequate support for the child to keep out of an unmanageable and unsolvable conflict. The ensuing desensitization led to the introjection of, and identification with that very conflict, and in turn to an externalization which transformed every contact situation into a potential threat.

Even when he succeeded in mobilizing his voice on his own behalf, it was mainly in the service of keeping out of reach, of escaping from some imposition or responsibility that might possibly be put on him. He was most emphatic in saying, "I can't!", "I am not able to ... ", "I don't know!" The tone of his voice left no doubt that what he was really expressing was, "I won't!" But he had found a technique by which he did not have to realize, and therefore did not have to feel guilty about, his own spitefulness. It was comparatively easy to make the patient sensorially and intellectually aware of *what* he was doing, *what* he was doing it *for*, that his techniques provided *support for withdrawal* from undesirable and unmanageable experiences in the *past*, that they *now* constituted a blockage and *interference with the desired contact*. It was very laborious and took many months of concentration and a great number of experiments and exercises around every detail of his withdrawal techniques to get the patient to that degree of motoric awareness where he became able to make a relevant change.

If in the case of Claudia we found a certain mobility of the extremities unsupported by the more central coordination of posture and breathing, in Walter we found hardly any mobility at all. He was all in one piece, literally pulled together. Claudia had the possibility of comparing the rigidity of her back, chest and pelvis with the jerkiness of the extremities, and consequently she could experiment with the extension of both modes of moving in either direction, until she had achieved some

continuity of coordination and flexibility. But Walter had
nothing to compare, i.e., there was not enough difference
in his motoric experience to make any particular movement or tension foreground figure, nothing except the
shrug of the shoulders. From the awareness of the shoulder shrug, the stocktaking expanded. The patient experienced the comparative mobility of the shoulders as
against the rigidity of the adjoining regions, neck, arms,
chest. He spontaneously realized the shrugging not just
as a symbolic gesture, but as an actual motoric expression
of "I can't!", "I don't know!", the onset of a movement
without reach, without direction, without continuity.
Experimenting with reach, continuity and direction, the
patient realized that he did not make any outgoing movements at all, that he was completely pulled together in the
vertical, and had no expansion whatsoever in the horizon-
tal direction, no flexibility of the neck, no swing or lift in
his arms, no buoyancy, no stance, no stride.

When, after several months of awareness experiments and exercises, he had partially succeeded in loosen-
ing up, his dutiful schoolboy attitude ("my wife thinks ...
my analyst says ... I know I should ... ") changed to real
interest and curiosity. He became easier with people and
much friendlier. At this stage he went through a period
of intense embarrassment. He was encouraged to admit
and express the embarrassment rather than to withdraw
from the embarrassing situations or, worse, to stick them
out with grim determination. It was pointed out that
embarrassment is the inevitable awareness of lack of
support that accompanies the initial exciting contact with
any new experience. Thus it is the emotional state apply-

ing to all stages of rapid growth and development. It is typical for the small child at a certain stage as well as for the adolescent. It is due to a lack or an unawareness of adequate techniques to cope with the new experience. If one can stay with the situation in spite or, or better *with*, the embarrassment, he has a chance, by discovering and developing new support attitudes, to make more successful contact with the new experience and thus to overcome the embarrassment. If, on the other hand, one avoids the embarrassment either by withdrawing from possibly embarrassing situations (like Walter) or by brazening them out with a pretended courage (like Claudia), he will never acquire new valid support techniques, i.e., he will have to confine his contact experiences either in fact (like Walter) or in sensitivity and consequence (like Claudia).

For several weeks Walter felt and behaved like an adolescent; he blushed and giggled and his voice changed. In a few instances, when the discrepancy between his new involvement and the lack of support, mainly the rigidity in his diaphragm and his upper arms, became too overwhelming, he became quite hysterical, laughing and crying and wildly gesticulating. He was afterwards able to recognize the attack as the spontaneous mobilization of these most inflexible and insensitive parts of his organism (the hysterical attack is probably a motoric emergency reaction of the total organism, just as yawning is in the case of oxygen deficiency). Consequently he could extend this awareness into more and more coordinated mobility.

At this stage, *group therapy* became the most effective agent in the patient's development. At first he balked at even remotely considering the possibility of taking part in a group. But gradually he agreed, at least intellectually, that it might be a desirable step. Finally he joined, at first very shyly sitting on the fringe, a silent observer. He refused even to take the most minor part in any psycho-dramatic experiment. But soon, encouraged by his observation of other group members, he began to admit and express his own uneasiness and embarrassment.**

It was in the group situation that he became fully aware of how vigorously and emphatically he insisted on being ignorant and being incapable. He recognized it as a rather clever and, in its own way, competent avoidance technique. From here on it was only a few steps, via some experiments with direct mutual criticism among the group members and an exciting psychodramatic experi-ence where he acted his mother shouting, scolding, and slapping a little boy, to a greater realization of his own present-day contact with people, his own interests, opin-ions, criticisms, needs, demands.

With increasing self-awareness he simultaneously became more genuinely aware of others, too. He does not have to figure out any more what is expected of him, he responds immediately to the situation and resists vigorously when he feels imposed upon. He is intelligent-

---

**Again this is in contrast to Claudia who had to control and domi-nate the proceedings from the very beginning. When her brazenness and phoniness was attacked she had no support at all and could not face her embarrassment. She attended only very few meetings and dropped out of her group (1952) after one of the members had pointed out the senselessness of her hand-washing compulsion by showing her the dirt on her hands through a magnifying glass. A few weeks ago she returned to the group of her own accord, more interested, more observant, more cooperative.

ly helpful to anyone in need; to the great surprise of everybody he was the only one who, when one of the group members stormed out of the room in a fit of anger and tears, went the next day to visit her to find out if she was all right.

Today he is the "father" of the group, benevolent, a little reserved but not shy, dignified without being stuffy, critical without nagging, quite gay with a keen sense of humor. His family relationships have improved; he enjoys the children (the child's therapist is delighted with his patience and understanding); he shares more interests and experiences with his wife. His business contacts are much easier; he feels more confident and less apprehensive; his income during the last year has substantially increased. At present he is abroad, an honored house guest of someone whom formerly he was afraid of as his boss, but now appreciates as his client. He acts his age, and he looks ten years younger.

"Two Instances of Gestalt Therapy" originally appeared in Volume III (1956) of *Case Reports in Clinical Psychology*.

9.

One Gestalt Therapist's Approach

Confronted with the formidable list of questions that the Program Committee has set up, I am a very reluctant speaker. If this grand inquisitor were a *patient* coming for his first session with me armed with this type of question "what do you do, when ... ?" I would not try to answer a single one. Instead I might tell him a story.

Two beggars, a blind man and a fool, are traveling together. At the end of a long, hot day they come to a farmhouse and the fool says: "Let's go in and ask for a glass of milk." The blind one asks: "What is milk?" "Milk? Milk is white." "What is white?" "White? White is a swan." "But what is a swan?" "A swan is a large bird with a bent neck." "And what is 'bent'?" The fool takes the blind one's arm, straightens it out and says: "You see? This is straight. And this," he bends the other one's arm at the wrist and elbow: "this is 'bent'." "Aaahh," says the blind man, "now I know what milk is!"

So let us go begging together and try to answer the first question: *What to do with the reluctant patient?*

All patients are reluctant about something or other, some time or other. Almost all patients are poorly motivated in the sense that they come, or are made to come, for the wrong reasons. I am suspicious of the patient who shows a great deal of insight and wears his suffering on the tip of his tongue. And I am wary of the overeager, enthusiastically cooperative patient who agrees and confirms, picks up the jargon in a jiffy, and dreams to order. He is reluctant to experience and express his difference of opinion, his doubts and objections.

But altogether, I am not particularly interested in the questions of motivation and referral. I take the patient as he presents himself at the time of his session with me. He was motivated enough to come for that appointment, and we take it from there, making contact with one another strictly on the basis of our mutual awareness at the time. Focusing on *what is* rather than on *what is not* or *what should be* usually gives the patient sufficient support to come for the next session — not necessarily a better motivation for "having therapy," but the willingness to continue contact with the therapist.

I have made home calls only in cases of immobilizing accidents and in two cases of agoraphobia. After a few weeks both patients were able to come to my office.

The patient who forgets or refuses to pay your fees will give indications of his reluctance right from the beginning of therapy not only in respect to money, but to anything else that you may ask of him: punctuality for appointments, information, expression of opinions and feelings, attempting an experiment, evaluation of his own or other people's attitudes and actions. He may be reluctant for many reasons: fear or spite, a confused sense of values, an infantile need to be cared for without having to do anything in return. These are the problems which ultimately must be tackled. In the meantime, of course, the patient can be coaxed and prodded into paying reluctantly, one way or another (you can make it clear that whatever you do for or with him cannot be evaluated and compensated for in money. What the patient pays for is your time and your attention during that time. Everything that takes place during the session is in the service of the *patient's* needs, even those of our demands which at the time make him anxious or uncomfortable. For his own needs the therapist asks only the regular payment). This explanation is usually intellectually accepted as fair, but you will find that the patient's reluctance changes into genuine willingness to pay only when he has developed an awareness of his own value. Only he can *give* who *has* and *is*.

On the other hand, the easily and regularly paying patient is not necessarily the most promising one. He may get some secret satisfaction from his family's sacrifices for him. He may be *buying you off.*

He may even be the *window-shopping* patient who precisely does *not "buy,"* but pays the admission fee for a consultation as for a fashion show, tries out the analyst for size, and repeats the same stunt during the next season of confusion or depression with another therapist. I find that my awareness of the patient's "style," and the fact that I show him only what *immediately* "fits" him, usually makes him "buy." So I get stuck finally with the window shopper, saddled not only with his "reluctance" but also with the particular problems accruing from his former abortive attempts at therapy. But this is another story!

The second question: *Do you assume that you unconsciously want every one of your patients to get better?*

I cannot answer. I don't know what I do unconsciously. As far as I am *aware*, I want my patients to get better. If they don't, I have to search for what I have failed to become aware of or to make *them* realize in the ongoing relationship.

For this I have to make use not only of their expressions, communications, and attitudes, but also of my so-called counter-transference. I do not like to use this term, which does not make sense in our approach in that takes its bearings from the awareness of the actual present moment and not from the interpretation of the past.

I do not always *verbally* express my feelings and attitudes toward the patient. But in the course of the therapy the patient learns to become aware of my reactions and expressions just as much (and sometimes more so!) as I am aware of his, even if not verbalized.

I share verbally only that much of *my* awareness that will enable him to take the next step in his own —

that will expand his support for taking a risk in the context of his actual present malfunction. If I communicate *too* much, I may provoke a *negative* therapeutic reaction: intolerable anxiety, flight, resistance, paralysis, desensitization, projection.

I will describe some problems and experiences from my own life or from other *cases*, if I expect this to give support to the patient for a fuller realization of his own position and potentialities — if it may help him to make the next step.

The third question: *What to do with the "acting out" patient?*

This seems to me to *create* a problem rather than to pinpoint one. Every patient, all the time, is *acting* in *some* way, and we call it "acting out" mainly when it is obviously undesirable, inadequate, exaggerated, overaggressive, perverted, e.g., when it interrupts the patient's ongoing development and relationships. But the patient is or may be "acting out" also when he behaves very correctly — holds a catatonic pose — and frequently even when he verbalizes most rationally and articulately; and he will continue to "act out" as long as he has insufficient support for more appropriate behavior. So the task of therapy is not to interfere in or prevent the patient's "acting out," which is for him anyhow the only *possible* way to *act*, but to build up more adequate self-support for more continuously integrating and integrated behavior.

This time-consuming process is usually not aided by the imposition of all kinds of restrictions, limitations and threats, at least not as far as the patient's behavior outside the therapy situation is concerned. Within the therapy situations some restrictions can be part of an experimental exploration of the patient's behavioral patterns and possibilities; but it is the *patient's* reaction that sets the limitations of tolerance of *therapist* behavior.

I am not punitive. I don't think that the attitude: "you better do what I am telling you, or else ... !" goes with a genuine respect for the patient, whose resistances are his main support. To punish him for what he relies on most, always provokes a negative reaction: fear, spite, resentment, vindictiveness, all of which interrupt the ongoing process of communication and understanding. The punitive therapist is himself "acting out" in the worst possible way; and he does so for the same reason as the "acting out" patient: because he does *not know* what else to do, because he *himself* has not enough support to give support where it is most needed.

The fourth question: *physical contact with the patient?*

I shall answer very briefly. I use any sort of physical contact if I expect it to facilitate the patient's next step in his awareness of the actual situation and what he is doing (or not doing) in and with it. I have no special rules with regard to male or female patients. I will light a cigarette, feed someone with a spoon, fix a girl's hair, hold hands, or hold a patient on my lap, if that appears to be the best means of establishing the nonexistent or interrupted communication. I also touch patients or let them touch *me* in experiments to increase body-awareness:

to point out tensions, malcoordination, rhythm of breathing, jerkiness or fluidity of motion, etc., etc.

There seems to be great divergence of opinion and a lot of anxiety about the admissibility of physical contact in therapy, as is indicated by the very phrasing of the questions we are considering here. They look to me very much like a plea for safe conduct through uncharted territory, obviously an absurdity. If we want to help our patients to realize themselves more fully as truly *human* beings, we ourselves must have the courage to risk the dangers of being human.

This brings me straight to the question: *What do you think about the basic nature of man, and how does this affect the therapy process?*

I am sorry that this has been put as the *last* question, for I consider it the *most important* one, in the light of which all the others either make sense or are irrelevant. I believe that not only every therapeutic measure, but every single thought and act, is informed by our basic conviction of what makes man "human," even if we never manifestly express this conviction and take it so much for granted that we are hardly aware of it ourselves. Speaking strictly for myself — the only way a Gestalt therapist can say anything at all — I am deeply convinced that the basic problem of *life*, not only of *therapy*, is: How to make life *livable* for a being whose dominant characteristic is his awareness of himself as a unique individual on the one hand, of his mortality, on the other. The first gives him a feeling of overwhelming importance as the very center of the world, the other a feeling of frustration and vanity, being less than a grain of sand in the Universe. Suspended between these two poles he vibrates in a state of inevitable tension and anxiety that, at least to modern western man, seems unrelievable and has given rise to various neurotic solutions. If the awareness and expression of uniqueness and individuality is repressed, we have the uniformity, boredom and ultimate meaninglessness of mass culture, in which the awareness of one's own dying becomes so intolerable that it has to be alienated at any price, by "having fun" with accumulated inanities or with artificial excitements (alcohol, dope, delinquency). When uniqueness and individuality are *over*-emphasized, we have a false "humanism" with man as the measure of all things, resulting in exaggerated expectations, frustration, and disappointment. As a reaction-formation, we find either a false detachment, a hopeless or blasé laissez-faire, or a false commitment, a frantic pursuit of a pseudo-creativeness, which is only an obsessional fiddling around with "hobbies" and "cultural activities," from do-it-yourself painting of the kitchen shelves to "seeing my analyst" and going to church.

Real creativeness, in my experience, is inextricably linked with the awareness of mortality. The sharper this awareness, the greater the urge to bring forth something new, to participate in the infinitely continuing creativeness in nature. This is what makes out of sex, love; out of the herd, society; out of corn and fruit, bread and wine; and out of sound, music. This is what makes life livable and — incidentally — therapy possible.

As long as the Judeo-Christian orientation was the structural mainstay of society and personality, western man could accept the identity of living and dying without questioning. In the East, the aim of Zen Buddhism is precisely this realization of identity of living and dying, of commitment and detachment. In our western world, the neurotic is the man who cannot face his own dying and therefore cannot fully live as a human being.

In Gestalt therapy, with its emphasis on immediate awareness and involvement, we have a method for developing the necessary support-functions for a self-continuing creative adjustment which is the only way of coping with the experience of dying and, therefore, of living.

"One Gestalt Therapist's Approach" was presented in New York City as a paper at the 1959 annual conference of the American Academy of Psychotherapists. It was published as "The Gestalt Approach" in Barron & Harper's (Eds.) *Annals of Psychotherapy* in 1962 and was revised for publication Fagan & Sheperd's (Eds.) *Gestalt Therapy Now* in 1970.

10.

Notes on Anxiety and Fear

Fear is of otherness; of an object, a person, a recognizable event. It mobilizes increased attention (orientation) for and manipulation of the dangerous situation.

The metabolism increases: excitement, anger, aggressiveness.

Fear and courage are not mutually exclusive phenomena, but manifestations of one and the same experience: *contact with danger.* Heightened awareness and the temporary surplus production of energy facilitate an extraordinary manipulation of a situation. So the "courageous" deed does not appear as anything very special to the "modest" hero.

In contrast, *anxiety* arises within a confluence situation, whenever and wherever the confluence is threatened. The threat remains essentially vague, as a tendency toward a break – arising either in the individual itself or in its environment – cannot be objectively recognized within a state of confluence.

The *state of confluence* is a system of organismic balance which is supposed to function without specifically awares orientation and specifically directed manipulation. Whenever this balance is upset, there is anxiety.

Anxiety is the *only earliest infantile emotion*. (Its alternative is *indifference*, when the confluence balance is one hundred percent functioning.) It is a state of general undifferentiated irritation which does not provide sufficient orientation for a successful coping with the situation.

Anxiety as a predominantly infantile emotion can be adequately managed and overcome in early infancy only with purely infantile means. The undifferentiated irritation is discharged in undifferentiated, undirected motoric reactions: crying and kicking, which in turn is normally sufficient to promote some kind of activity in the environment which restores the balance. I don't think that an infant can be paralyzed by anxiety. And no adult in full possession of support and contact functions is paralyzed by fear.

Paralysis is the inhibition of a potentially inadequate manipulation combined with faulty or inadequate orientation. In this state of half-orientation there is a dim "self-conscious" awareness of the responsibility of motoric activity for whatever changes in the situation. The first *awareness is of the break of confluence*, which one's own already recognized activity must be responsible for – as the boundary between one's own and anyone else's

activity is not yet established or not adequately functioning (shock, drugs, exhaustion, introjection, projection,
etc.). Thus the paralysis appears as a kind of magic
gesture, an attempt to prevent or ignore the disastrous
event — the break of confluence — and one's *own quilt
feelings*.

The following diagram may illustrate more clearly
the coordination of the different phases of orientation
and manipulation with the respective emotional reaction
to a threatening upset of balance.

ORIENTATION	MANIPULATION	EMOTIONAL RESPONSE
No orientation	Undifferentiated, undirected motor-ic activity	Anxiety, confluence
Inadequate, half-orientation, no more conflu-ence, not yet contact	Inadequate, half-directed motoric activity: motoric block clumsiness paralysis mistakes	Embarrassment Guilt feeling Self-consciousness Panic Fear
Full, adequate, orientation; contact	Specific organized motoric activity	Courage

If we look for the survival values of these different reactions, we can make the following observations: The expression of anxiety, e.g., the display of helplessness and unorganized motor activity, evokes compassion, sympathy from the environment, and with it a restoration of balance. It is, therefore, at least for the infant, an adequate reaction. Its value for the grown-up is minimal, for what promotes sympathy and assistance for the small child may provoke antipathy, ridicule, and rejection for the adult, particularly if the anxiety and disorganization applies only to certain fields of experience (phobia), while within other fields the patient may show quite adequate orientation and manipulation.

The advanced psychotic may be slightly better off in regard to eliciting sympathy from the environment, as his anxiety may be as obvious and all-pervading as an infant's. But while the small child's unrecognized specific needs are comparatively primitive and can be more or less easily and specifically surmised by an experienced environment, the unrealizable specific needs of the adult psychotic are much more complicated not only by his more differentiated adult structure, but by introjections and projections that can hardly ever be completely gauged, let alone satisfied, by even the most experienced and sympathetic environment, and so his anxiety is never completely assuaged.

"Notes on Anxiety and Fear" was originally prepared for presentation to the New York Institute for Gestalt Therapy in 1965. It appears here in English for the first time.

11.

Some Aspects of Gestalt Therapy

Many years ago I had a dream that is present with me whenever I am asked to write a paper or to speak *ex cathedra* as an "authority" on the theory and practice of Gestalt therapy.

The night before the dream I read a poem by John Crowe Ransom called "The Equilibrists." It closes with the line: "Let them lie perilous and beautiful."

In my dream I am walking along the beach where I meet Paul Goodman and his son Mathew. They are collecting shells and pebbles. I say:

> Don't gather them; when they get dry
> The shells will break, the pebbles grow gray
> And dull.
> Let them lie perilous and beautiful.

This is my existence: I am Paul and Mathew, the teacher and the student, the observer and the categorizer. I am the shells and pebbles, fragile and dull when stranded and at the mercy of the scientists and curio collectors. I am the beach, the ever-moving shoreline where the dry past is periodically revitalized and augmented or diminished by the waves of the present. I am also the sea, the continually self-renewing rhythmically moving vital force. And I am the poet who knows something that the scientists have forgotten.

I have just given you a somewhat abridged example of dreamwork in Gestalt therapy. What I came to realize through working with this dream, and what I am trying to tell you particularly in its application to the questions that we are confronted with today, is that the dry-sorting out and summarizing of the Gestalt experience into the pigeonholes labeled Theory, Techniques, Amplifications, and Expectations of Accomplishment is entirely out of tune with the holistic and organismic philosophy of Gestalt.

I like to think of any theory, including Gestalt, more as a working hypothesis, an auxiliary construct that we build and adhere to for purposes of communication, rationalization, and justification of our particular personal approach. These semantic constructs, if they are in themselves continuous and coherent, can be, as is the work of Freud, great works of art and as such valid expressions of, and support for, the experience and development of many people within a certain cultural situation. But, like any fixed gestalt, they may under different circumstances become a definite block in the development of a person, a relationship, a group, or a whole culture.

This brings me straight to the, for me, basic postulate in Gestalt therapy, the *awareness continuum*, the freely *ongoing gestalt formation*, where whatever happens to be of greatest concern to a person, a relationship or a group, comes into the foreground where it can be contacted and coped with, so that then it can go into the background and leave the foreground free for the next relevant gestalt.

Contact is made in any actual *present situation*, the only moment in which experience and change are possible. Whenever we think and talk of the past, our memories, regrets, resentments, grief, or nostalgia occur and are relevant right here and now, in the present. Whenever we talk about the future, we are fantasizing, planning, hoping, expecting, conspiring, looking forward to or dreading from where we are here and now, in the present situation. *Gestalt therapy* is an *existential, experiential, and experimental* approach which takes its bearings from *what is, not from what has been or what should be.* No interpretation is necessary as we work with what is available in the actual present awareness of patient and therapist and what becomes possible to experiment with through this ever-increasing awareness.

Contact is a *boundary phenomenon* between organism and environment. It is the acknowledgement of, and the coping with, the *other*. The boundary where I and the other meet is the locus of the ego functions of identification and alienation, the sphere of excitation, interest, concern and curiosity, or fear and hostility.

The *elasticity of the boundary* equals the *awareness continuum*: if there is no interference with sensoric and motoric functions, there is a ceaselessly ongoing exchange and growth (Carl Whitaker calls it the growing edge) and a continuous expansion of the common ground for communication.

When the *boundaries* become *fixed*, we have at best the *obsessional* personality, the strong "character" with fixed attitudes and habits, who lives righteously by law and order, principles, pride, and prejudice. At worst, we get the catatonic who may suddenly burst out of his confinement in an uncontrollable and destructive rage.

When the boundaries are broken or blurred, the door is open for introjection and projection. At best we have the infantile hanger-on, the greedy introjector for whom happiness is identical with a state of complete confluence, who experiences the other as threatening and hostile. At worst, we have the emotionally indifferent, disoriented schizophrenic whose communication is either bizarre or nonexistent and who may degenerate into a completely alienated and isolated nonperson.

Contact is possible only to the extent that *support for* it is available. *Support* is the total background against which the present experience stands out (exists) and forms a meaningful gestalt. For this is what meaning is: the relation of a figure to its ground.

Support is everything that facilitates the ongoing assimilation and integration of experience for a person, a relationship or a society: primary physiology, upright posture and coordination, sensitivity and mobility, language, habits and customs, social manners and relationships, and everything else that we have acquired and learned during our lifetime; in short, everything that we usually take for granted and rely on, even and particularly our hang-ups and resistances — the fixed ideas, ideals and behavior patterns which have become second nature precisely because they were supportive at the time of their formation. When they have outlived their usefulness, they become blocks in the ongoing life process. We are stuck, at an impasse, in a double bind, a deathlike paralysis.

In Gestalt therapy we de-automatize these secondary automatisms by staying with the apparently insoluble conflict and exploring every available detail: muscular tensions, the resulting desensitization, the rationalizations, the investment in the status quo, the introjections and projections, etc., etc. With increasing awareness and the concomitant insights, resensitization and remobilization, alternatives become possible and available. The *impasse turns into a present problem* that we can cope with and take responsibility for here and now.

This brings us to the question of *techniques*. As a Gestalt therapist I prefer to speak of *styles* as a unified way of expression and communication. In Gestalt therapy there are as many styles as there are therapists and patients. A *therapist applies himself* in and to a situation with whatever life experience and professional skills have become assimilated and integrated as his background, which give meaning to his and the patient's present awareness. He continually surprises not only his patients and groups, but also himself.

Therapy in itself is an *innovative process* in which patient and therapist continually discover themselves and each other and ongoingly invent their relationship.

It is rather unfortunate that through the extensive demonstrations and film work of Fritz Perls only the approach he used in his last three or four years has become widely known as Gestalt therapy. His dream work is being imitated as "the" Gestalt technique and misused in a mechanical, simplistic, and gimmicky way by many untrained and inexperienced group leaders. But imitators with no regard for the complexities in a situation and with no awareness of the patients and their own limitations are not only ignorant, but inauthentic and irresponsible.

There are no amplifications in Gestalt therapy techniques. Gestalt therapy in itself is a continually ongoing amplification with whatever means happen to be available in whatever direction is possible and desirable.

I personally work a lot with body awareness: breathing, posture, coordination, continuity and fluidity in movement; with gestures, facial expressions, voice, and language and its particular idiosyncratic uses. I'll work with a musician at his instrument and with a writer on his manuscript. I work with dreams and fantasies to facilitate the identification or re-identification with alienated or undeveloped parts of the personality.

I work with the *obvious*, with what is immediately accessible to the patient's or my own awareness. Ironically, we use the Latin word "obvious" as indicative of something that is too easy and trivial to bother about; and the Greek word "problem" in the opposite sense: a most serious difficulty that has to be worried about, diagnosed, worked through, solved, overcome, etc. But linguistically both words have exactly the same meaning, namely, what is right in front of you, right in your way. The therapeutic possibilities in an occasional reversal of our usage are too obvious to even talk about!

I also don't want to talk about Achievements. In Gestalt therapy we encourage and facilitate the ongoing process of awareness of and coping with *what is*, and we terminate therapy when the patient experiences that degree of integration that facilitates its own development.

"Some Aspects of Gestalt Therapy" was presented as a paper at the 1972 meeting of the Mid-Atlantic Group Therapy Association which met in Washington D.C.. It was published in German in 1979 in the *Gestalt-Bulletin.*

12.

Comments
on
the
New
Directions

The German word "Gestalt" is untranslatable into a single English term. It covers a multitude of related concepts like countenance, shape, form, figure, configuration, structural entity, a whole that is something more than, or different from, the sum of its parts. A Gestalt stands out from the background, it "exists," and the relationship of a figure to its ground is what we call "meaning." If this relationship is tenuous or nonexistent, or if, for whatever reasons (cultural, educational), we are unable to recognize and understand it, we say: "It doesn't make sense." It is absurd, bizarre, meaningless.

Whatever exists is here and now. The past exists now as memory, nostalgia, regret, resentment, fantasy, legend, history. The future exists here and now in the actual present as anticipation, planning, rehearsal, expectation and hope, or dread and despair. Gestalt therapy takes its bearing from *what is* here and now, not from what *has been* or what *should be*. It is an existential-phenomenological approach, and as such it has to be experiential and experimental. Thus talking "about" Gestalt therapy is really quite contrary to the philosophy of Gestalt.

The *actual experience* of any present situation does not need to be explained or interpreted; it can be directly contacted, felt and described here and now. Gestalt therapy deals with the obvious, with what is *immediately* available to the awareness of client or therapist and can be shared and expanded in the actual ongoing communication. The aim of Gestalt therapy is the *awareness continuum*, the freely ongoing gestalt formation where what is of greatest concern and interest to the organism, the relationship, the group or society becomes Gestalt, comes into the foreground where it can be fully experienced and coped with (acknowledged, worked through, sorted out, changed, disposed of, etc.) so that then it can melt into the background (be forgotten or assimilated and integrated) and leave the foreground free for the next relevant gestalt.

Any *fixed* gestalt in time becomes a block. In psychoanalytic terms, one would speak of complexes, inhibitions, and resistances, and look for their origin and causes in past early experience. But the fixation is not *on* and *in* the *past*; it is right here and now in the still activated muscular tensions, the habitual and automatic behavior patterns and social attitudes which have become second nature. Automatisms save energy and are useful when they support the ongoing life process. In Gestalt therapy we work through the resistances of de-automatizing those behavior patterns which have become impediments by bringing them into the foreground where they can be experienced again as conscious activities that the patient can then take responsibility for: "This is what *I* am doing. What does that do for me? Do I want to do that now? What else could I do?" With the increased awareness of *how? where? when? to what extent?*, the *why?* either becomes self-evident or unimportant. We can experiment with alternatives here and now, and change becomes possible.

The fixed gestalt as a block applies not only in personal, social and scientific development. I see it also and particularly in the theories and practice of psycho-therapy. I think of any theory (including Gestalt) not as holy script but rather as a working hypothesis, a service-able device for the description, communication, and rationalization of our particular personal approach. And in practice I would rather speak of *style*, a unified integrat-ed way of expression and communication, than of definite prescribed techniques. The experiments are not fixed constellations of technical steps, but invented *ad hoc* to facilitate awareness of *what is*. Fritz Perls — with a pre-psychiatry history of interest and active involvement in the theater — would use a psycho-dramatic approach. Other Gestalt therapists work with art, music, poetry, philoso-phy, meditation, yoga, and other body awareness methods like sensitivity training, modern dance, Alexander and Rolfing techniques, bio-energetics, Arica training, eye exercises, and whatever else they have assimilated and integrated into their total functioning. So it is not Gestalt therapy *and* body awareness, or Gestalt therapy *and* art, or

Gestalt therapy *and* something else, but Gestalt therapy in itself as a continually ongoing innovation and expansion in whatever direction is possible and with whatever means are available between therapist and patient in the actual therapeutic situation.

It is unfortunate that what has become very widely known and practiced as Gestalt therapy is only the method used by my late husband for demonstration workshops and films in the last three or four years of his life. The dramatization of dreams, identifying with and acting through every part of the dream, is an immensely impressive demonstration method, and Fritz Perls used it with a skill and sensitivity that was informed by 70 years of experience. Imitating his method as "the" therapeutic technique without full regard for the specific needs and limitations in the actual situation is superficial, simplistic, mechanical, manipulative, and unauthentic. A Gestalt therapist does not use techniques; he applies *himself in* and *to* a situation with whatever professional skill and life experience he has accumulated and integrated. There are as many styles as there are therapists and clients who discover themselves and each other and together invent their relationship.

In facilitating the awareness continuum, I find the experience and the concept of contact as the *boundary function* most useful, particularly in its application to education and child and family therapy. Contact is a boundary phenomenon between organism and environment. It is the acknowledgement of, and the coping with, the *other*, the not-me, the different, the strange. The boundary where I and the other meet is the locus of the ego functions of identification and alienation, the sphere of excitation, interest, concern, and curiosity, or of fear and hostility.

The *elasticity* of the boundary equals the awareness continuum. If there is no interference with the sensory and motoric functions, there is a ceaselessly ongoing exchange and growth on the boundary, the growing edge (as Carl Whitaker would call it), and a continuous expansion of the ground for communication.

A small child, before becoming socialized, lives on the boundary: looks at everything, touches everything, gets into everything. He discovers the world, expands his awareness and means of coping at his own pace: playfully serious or seriously playing, he makes an ongoing creative adjustment to his own potential. We all know how in the usual upbringing of children the ongoing spontaneous development and growth are systematically interfered with: Don't do this, don't touch that, don't answer back, don't be a crybaby, pull yourself together, etc., etc. This results in *self-interference*, the muscular tensions and contractions which Wilhelm Reich recognized as the character armor, the fixed attitudes, habits, and principles that pervade our whole culture and confine and define the so-called "*normal*," e.g. more or less obsessional, personality that is "well adjusted," lives rigidly and righteously by law and order, pride and prejudice, and remains ignorant of, hostile to, and isolated from anything and anyone beyond these fixed boundaries.

On the other hand, convention and conformity insist on a *confluent* attitude *within* the fixed boundaries, a taking for granted of sameness and agreement, of being *one* — a "we"-ness without the I and Thou — the acknowledgment of the other and oneself as separate individuals. This blurring and ignoring of boundaries apply not only to society at large and certain social, political, educational, and scientific or business organizations, but particularly to the interpersonal relationships in marriage and family. It is still largely taken for granted that husband and wife should be not only one flesh, but one mind and soul, they should have the same opinions, interests, involvements, friends. Differences are glossed over or ignored, and occasionally lead to a fight (where eventually they make *real contact*) in which the stronger partner usually asserts his (or her) superiority and restores the confluence. In confluence relationships the stronger partners have a greater chance to express their individuality. The weaker ones submit, hold back their disagreements and differences, and eventually become resentful and possibly spiteful, while the stronger partners become bored with the relationship, as no interesting stimulus or response can come from a partner who feels oppressed. Resentment and boredom are the very characteristics of the average marriage. Only when these couples are ready to split are the differences and recriminations finally expressed, often with great vindictiveness and violence.

The same difficulties apply, to an even greater extent, in the parent-child relationship. The embryo is *de facto* in complete organismic confluence with the mother. After birth, the infant breathes separately; but breathing is a primary automatism that the child remains unaware of. For nourishment and care the child remains confluent, e.g. experiences the mother and the caring environment not as separate but as an extension of himself. The contact functions, like coping with solid food, orientation, and manipulation develop only slowly in accordance with the development of the cortex, the visual, tactual, and aural recognition of people and objects, the muscular coordination in handling objects, and achieving upright posture and mobility.

On the other side, the *parents* tend to experience the child as an extension of themselves, the mother by maintaining the original confluence with the embryo and infant, both parents by investing in the child all their own unrealized desires, hopes, and ambitions. The child "belongs" to the family; and belonging means to be owned, having no separate existence, but being confined within the same boundaries and, of course, also being protected by them as long as the child becomes and remains adjusted. But while animals stop nursing their young so that they will learn to find their own food; while birds push their young out of the nest so that they will fly; while Australian aborigines send their adolescent boys into the wilderness where they have to prove that they can survive on their own, we in our culture keep our children longer and longer dependent, far beyond the age of actual physical and mental maturity, and expect them to remain confluent with family, school, and social establishment. When we succeed, we produce the infantile hanger-on, the greedy introjector who swallows indiscriminately what is stuffed down his throat and who can't stand on his own feet. When we fail, we get the reaction formation, the spiteful brat who says "no" to everything, remains undernourished, and becomes progressively more alienated and isolated. But conforming or spite are both two sides of the same coin: dependence. True independence is possible only with the experience of separateness *and* the ability to make contact with what is different. Confluence (within the *same* boundary) or isolation (away from the boundary) are not contact which is *on* the boundary. "Good fences make good neighbors."

We talk about being or staying in contact, having erratic or indifferent contact, or being out of contact. Now contact is nothing one *has*, or *is*, or *stays in* or *out* of. If we stay too long, we may end in confluence; if we withdraw too far, we end in isolation. It is not a state, but an activity with a certain rhythm of touching and letting go. We *make* contact by acknowledging and tackling the *other* and experiencing ourselves in doing so. It is a continuous shuttling or oscillating between *me* and the *other*, and no English or German or any other Caucasian language has an adequate word to describe it except the ancient Greek: *aisthesthai* — to be aware — is a medium form; grammatically it is passive, but it is used as an active verb. And, of course, full awareness implies the collaboration of all sensory and motoric functions.

Contact can be good and creative only to the extent that sufficient and adequate support for it is available. Any lack of essential support is experienced as anxiety. *Support* is everything that facilitates the ongoing assimilation and integration for a person, a relationship, or a society: primary physiology (like breathing and digestion), upright posture and coordination, sensitivity and mobility, language, habits and customs, social manners and relationships, and everything else that we have learned and experienced during our lifetime. In short, everything that we usually take for granted and rely on, even and particularly our hang-ups and resistances, the fixed ideas, ideals, and behavior patterns which have become second nature precisely because they were supportive at the time of their formation. When they have outlived their usefulness, they become blocks in the ongoing life process. We are stuck, in a bind, at an impasse.

In Gestalt therapy, we de-automatize these secondary automatisms by staying with the apparently insoluble conflict and exploring every available detail: the muscular tensions, the resulting desensitization, the rationalizations, the investment in the status quo, the introjections and projections, etc., etc. With increasing awareness and the concomitant insight, resensitization and remobilization *alternatives* become available and change becomes possible. The *impasse* turns into a *present problem* that we can cope with and take responsibility for here and now.

How we go about facilitating the awareness continuum and developing the support functions depends on what support we have in *ourselves* and on our awareness of what our client has available and what kind of support he is lacking. As I have said before, every Gestalt therapist develops his own style: I — with a background of music, eurythmics, modern dance, Eastern body approaches, and Eastern and Western existentialism, familiarity with several languages and their literature — work a lot with body awareness, with breathing, posture, coordination, continuity and fluidity in motion, with facial expression, gestures, voice. I work with speech patterns and the particular idiosyncratic uses of language. I work with dreams and fantasies to facilitate the identification with alienated or undeveloped parts of the personality. I'll quote from the Bible or Goethe, or tell a Zen story or a joke, if it will illuminate a dark corner in the patient's awareness. I'll work with a musician at his instrument and with a writer on his manuscript.

There are many more interesting and meaningful aspects of Gestalt therapy. Here and now I want to limit myself to the concepts and the experience of the awareness continuum, contact boundary, and support which, for me, form a coherent, very meaningful, strong gestalt, the very essence of Gestalt therapy.

"Comments on the New Directions" originally appeared in *The Growing Edge of Gestalt Therapy* which was edited by Edward W. L. Smith and first appeared in 1974. It appears here with Dr. Smith's kind permission.

13.

Concepts and Misconceptions of Gestalt Therapy

In Goethe's *Faust*, Mephistopheles says to an eager disciple:

> Denn eben wo Begriffe fehlen,
> Da stellt ein Wort zur rechten Zeit sich ein.
> (For, whenever there's a lack of concepts,
> There at the proper time a word comes
> handy.)

The Devil takes a hand in every human endeavor, not only in philosophy and theology. I see him at work in politics and education, in science and art, and particularly in our own field, the teaching and practice of psychotherapy, busily supplying not only words but ready-made formulas, techniques and gimmicks, a whole quick-change bag of tricks to whoever is needy, ignorant and credulous enough, and willing to pay.

The Devil is the master of short-cut, pretentious, seductive and deceiving, promising, coaxing, and relentlessly bullying. His tools are simplification, manipulation, and distortion.

Let us proceed now from myth to facts. At a meeting of the New York Institute for Gestalt Therapy, I put the question: What is your answer if somebody asks you: "What is Gestalt therapy?" Our Vice President, Richard Kitzler, who likes to play the Devil's advocate, mumbled under his breath: "The hot seat and the empty chair." Of course, like Mephisto, he said it tongue in cheek. But the naive and impatient disciple takes it at face value; he will always take the part for the whole.

The style that Fritz Perls developed in demonstration workshops for professionals during the last few years of his life has become widely known through films and videotapes of those workshops and through *Gestalt Therapy Verbatim* (1969), the transcripts of these tapes. The dramatization of dreams and fantasies is a beautiful demonstration method, particularly in workshops with professionals who have already had their personal analysis or therapy, and are themselves experienced in working with people. But it is only *one* aspect of the infinite possibilities in the Gestalt approach. It is not useful in working with very disturbed people and not usable at all with the real schizophrenic or paranoid patient. Fritz Perls knew this very well and simply bypassed workshop participants where he sensed the schizoid or paranoid disturbance.

Unfortunately, this workshop approach has become widely accepted as the essence of Gestalt therapy and applied by ever-growing numbers of therapists to whomever they are working with. Thus, Gestalt therapy is reduced to a purely *technical* modality which, because of its obvious limitations, then is combined with any other technical modality that happens to be available in the psychotherapeutic armamentarium. So we get sensitivity training *and* Gestalt, body awareness *and* Gestalt, Bioenergetics *and* Gestalt, art and dance therapies *and* Gestalt, Transcendental Meditation *and* Gestalt, Transactional Analysis *and* Gestalt, and something or other *and* Gestalt, ad infinitum.

All these combinations show that the basic concepts of Gestalt therapy are either misunderstood or simply not known. Gestalt therapy is neither a particular technique nor a collection of specific techniques. Thus, it is not an encounter or confrontation method with a structured sequence of directions, demands, and challenges. It is also not a dramatic-expressive method aimed primarily at the discharge of tension. Tension is energy, and energy is too costly a commodity to be simply discharged; it must be made available for effecting the necessary or desirable changes. The task of therapy is to develop sufficient support for the reorganization and rechanneling of energy

The basic concepts of Gestalt therapy are philosophical and aesthetic rather than technical. Gestalt therapy is an existential-phenomenological approach and as such it is experiential and experimental. Its emphasis on the Here and Now does not imply, as is often assumed, that past and future are unimportant or nonexistent for Gestalt therapy. On the contrary, the past is ever-present in our total life experience, our memories, nostalgia, or resentments, and particularly in our habits and hang-ups, in all the unfinished business, the fixed gestalten. The future is present in our preparations and beginnings, in expectation and hope, or dread and despair.

Why do we call our approach *Gestalt* therapy? "Gestalt" is a holistic concept (*ein Ganzheitsbegriff*). A gestalt is a structured entity that is more than, or different from, the sum of its parts. It is the foreground figure that stands out from its ground, it "exists." The term "Gestalt" entered the psychological vocabulary through the work of Wolfgang Koehler, who applied principles derived from field theory to problems of perception. Gestalt *psychology* was developed further by Max Wertheimer, Gelb and Goldstein, Koffka and Lewin, and their colleagues and students. For the development of Gestalt *therapy* the work of Wertheimer, Goldstein and Lewin became particularly important. Anybody who wants fully to understand Gestalt therapy would do well to study Wertheimer on productive thinking, Lewin on the incomplete gestalt and the crucial importance of interest for gestalt formation, and Kurt Goldstein on the organism as an indivisible totality.

Goldstein's organismic approach links up with Wilhelm Reich's theory of organismic self-regulation to become in Gestalt therapy the postulate of the awareness continuum, the freely ongoing gestalt-formation where whatever is of greatest interest and importance for the survival and development of the individual or social organism will become figure, will come into the foreground where it can be fully experienced and responsibly dealt with.

But Reich's most essential contribution to the development of Gestalt therapy is his recognition of the identity of muscular tensions and character formation. The character armor, epitomized in the obsessional character, is a fixed gestalt which becomes a block in the ongoing gestalt formation. The practical focus on body awareness, however, became part of Gestalt therapy not through Reich, but through my lifelong experience with eurythmics and modern dance, my early study of the work of Ludwig Klages, *Ausdrucksbewegung und Gestaltlungskraft* (expressive movement and creativity), and my awareness of Alexander and Feldenkrais methods long before the development of Bioenergetics and other body therapies. Working with breathing, posture, coordination, voice, sensitivity, and mobility became part of my therapeutic style already in the 1930s when we still called ourselves psychoanalysts.

The gradual shift from the psychoanalytical to a Gestalt orientation is documented in *Ego, Hunger and Aggression* (Perls, 1969), published first in 1942. I contributed to it two chapters that are predominantly Gestaltist: "The Dummy Complex," which is the *fixed gestalt* that prevents change, and "The Meaning of Insomnia," which is the *incomplete gestalt*, the unfinished situation which does not let us sleep. In *Ego, Hunger and Aggression* we changed from the historical-archaeological Freudian viewpoint to the existential-experiential, from piecemeal association psychology to a holistic approach, from the purely verbal to the organismic, from interpretation to direct awareness in the Here and Now, from transference to actual contact, from the concept of the Ego as a substance *having* boundaries to a concept of it as the very boundary phenomenon itself, *being* the actual *contact function* of identification and alienation. All these concepts, then still tentative, often confused and confusing, developed during the next ten years into a more organized coherent theory which was published as *Gestalt Therapy: Excitement and Growth in the Human Personality* (Perls, Goodman & Hefferline, 1951). This is the basic book that I still consider indispensable for a full understanding of Gestalt therapy.

However, at the risk of repeating what some of you have heard before, but what seems generally not well understood, I want to confine myself to a few concepts which are interconnected and, for me, essential for the theory *and* practice of Gestalt therapy: the concepts of boundary, contact and support.

Contact is the recognition of, and the coping with the *other*, the different, the new, the strange. It is not a state that we are in or out of (which would correspond more to the states of confluence or isolation), but an activity: I *make* contact on the boundary between me and the other. The boundary is where we touch and at the same time experience separateness. It is where the excitement is, the interest, concern, and curiosity or fear and hostility, where previously unaware or diffused experience comes into focus, into the foreground as a clear gestalt. The freely ongoing gestalt formation is identical with the process of growth, the creative development of self and relationship. If this continuum is interrupted by outside interference or blocked by the fixed gestalten of rigid character formation or of obsessional thoughts and activities, no strong new gestalt can emerge. The boundary experience becomes blurred and even wiped out by the fixed and incomplete gestalten. Excitement changes into anxiety and dread or indifference and boredom. The faculties of differentiation and discrimination are disowned and projected; attitudes, ideas, and principles of other people are misappropriated and introjected; energy that might be available for direct and creative action is deflected into dummy activities or retroflected in self-interference, self-reproachs, self-pity, and self-destruction. For a more detailed phenomenology of introjection, projection, deflection, and retroflection, I recommend Erving and Miriam Polster's book *Gestalt Therapy Integrated* (1973). How does a Gestalt therapist cope with this pandemonium of neurotic and psychotic pathology that we are faced with every day? Our aim is the awareness continuum, the freely flowing ongoing gestalt formation, which can go on only when excitement and interest can be maintained. Contact can be relevant and creative only to the extent that support for it is available. By support I mean only to the smallest degree the care and assurance that I as the therapist provide through my availability and interest, but the self-support that the patient (or the therapist, for that matter!) either relies on or is lacking. Support starts with primary physiology like breathing, circulation, and digestion, continues with the development of the cortex, the growing of teeth, upright posture, coordination, sensitivity and mobility, language and its uses, habits and customs, even and particularly the hang-ups which were formed as support at the time of their formation. All the experience and learning that has been *fully assimilated and integrated* builds up a person's background, which gives meaning to the emerging gestalten and thus supports a certain way of living *on* the boundary *with* excitement. Whatever is not assimilated either gets lost or remains an introject, a block in the ongoing development.

The integrated personality has *style*, a unified way of expression and communication. He or she may not conform to what is regarded as "well adjusted," socially useful and desirable, or even healthy. He will be called "eccentric" or "irresponsible," "queer," "crazy," or "criminal;" he may be an anarchist, a painter or poet, a homosexual or a hobo. But the person who has *style* does not come for therapy, at least not voluntarily. The people who want and need therapy are the ones who are stuck with their anxiety, their dissatisfaction, their inadequacies in work and relationships, their unhappiness. They lack support for the kind of contact that would be necessary or desirable and adequate to the situation they find themselves in.

Now any lack of essential support is experienced as anxiety. Usually anxiety is equated with insufficient oxygen, but the reduction and even suspension of breathing and with it a reduction of excitement and interest may already be a reaction formation to a potentially dangerous situation (playing possum) or to the demand for "self-control." There is a whole scale of malcoordinations of support and contact functions ranging from occasional unease, awkwardness, and embarrassment to chronic anxiety and panic. We have not enough time to go into the whole phenomenology of these malcoordinations. I only want to emphasize one point: awkwardness and embarrassment are potentially creative states, the temporary lack of balance we experience at the growing edge where we have one foot on familiar and one foot on unfamiliar ground, the very boundary experience itself. If we have mobility and allow ourselves to wobble, we can maintain the excitement, ignore and even forget the awkwardness, gain *new* ground and with it more support. We can see this graceful awkwardness in every small child before it becomes socialized and constrained by the civilized demand to "keep it cool." I know from my own experience how difficult it is to rid ourselves of the introjects that we have remained encumbered with through most of our lives. At this point, I feel nearly always a little awkward and embarrassed. Right now I feel a bit uneasy not exactly knowing whom I am talking to and rather talking *at* you. But I also know that I'll survive it. I have learned to live with *uncertainty without anxiety*.

How we do facilitate this development of more elastic support functions in our *patients* depends on the support we have in ourselves and our awareness of what is available in our clients. A good therapist does not use techniques, he applies himself in and to a situation with whatever knowledge, skills, and total life experience have become integrated into his own background and whatever awareness he has at any given moment. Thus, I would speak of *styles* of therapy rather than techniques. Nearly any technical modality is applicable within the framework of Gestalt therapy, if it is existential, experiential, and experimental only to the degree that support can be mobilized, e.g., if the patient is already or can be made aware of what and how he is doing now and willing to experiment with expansions or alternatives. So we start with the obvious, with what is immediately available to the awareness of therapist as well as client, and we proceed from there in small steps which are immediately experienced and thus are more easily assimilable. This is a time-consuming process which sometimes is misunderstood by people who are out for easy excitement and magical results. But miracles are a result not only of intuition, but of timing. I feel suspicious of the miracle worker and am weary of the instant breakthrough. More often than not, it results in a negative therapeutic reaction, a relapse, or even a psychotic break. It shows a lack of respect for the patient's existential predicament, not accepting him as he is at this moment, but manipulating him quickly to where we think he should be. It does not contribute to the development of his awareness and his autonomy, nor does it contribute to the growth of the therapist.

References

Perls, F., Hefferline, R. F., & Goodman, P. 1951. *Gestalt therapy: Excitement and growth in the human personality*. New York: Dell Publishing Co., Inc.

Perls, F. 1988. *Gestalt therapy verbatim.* Highland, New York: The Gestalt Journal.

Perls, F. 1969. *Ego, hunger, and aggression.* New York: Random House.

Polster, E. & M. 1973. *Gestalt therapy integrated.* New York: Brunner/Mazel.

"Conceptions and Misconceptions of Gestalt Therapy" was originally delivered as a talk to the European Association for Transactional Analysis which met in Seefeld, Austria in 1977. It was later published in Volume 14, Number 3, (1978) of *Voices.*

14.

A Workshop with Laura Perls

LAURA PERLS: The perception of reality is the awareness of what is, and what is depends on whatever you bring to a situation in yourself and whatever happens to be available in the situation. It depends on interest and availability. Right now I am aware of the shifting of attention; and now I am aware of a lot of faces, of whom I knew one or two before, and all the others are somewhat strange and you all look more or less expectant. What do you expect?

BILL: I'm feeling very happy to be with you again, Laura, very happy. I feel tears coming to my eyes. It's been a long time, ten years maybe, since before Fritz was gone.

LAURA: So you are aware more of your memory than of what is right here?

BILL: Memory in the here and now, side by side. The learning I had from you and Fritz comes back to me, fine memories. I'm happy to be here again, very happy. Side by side.

LAURA: So you look very sad.

BILL: I don't feel sad. My tears are tears of joy.

LAURA (to group): Don't leave it all to me.

JEAN: You have so much energy.

LAURA: How do you know?

JEAN: Because I see it.

LAURA: What do you see?

JEAN: Energy emanating from you. You have a sparkle in your eyes, a good muscle tone.

LAURA: I also don't feel very much at ease right now. I am, as I said, faced with a lot of new people and that is really the situation on the boundary, where I and the other meet. The boundary concept is really crucial in Gestalt therapy. That is where awareness takes place. That is where the excitement and the interest is and that is also where the unease and the embarrassment may be, the insecurity, the uncertainty, and if one can't tolerate that uncertainty it turns into anxiety. If you try to cover it up then either you have to withdraw, because you feel too anxious, or you try to brazen it out with grim determination and then you make an insensitive contact. Contact is on the boundary, and in order to make contact with a really new, different other you have to have enough support of it, and for me that is another crucial concept. One always talks about contact, making contact, and being in contact and having good contact or erratic contact or no contact, but contact can be only as good as support is available. And by support I don't mean just my presence as a group leader or as a therapist, my availability, but what the patient or the client or the trainee brings to the situation. Support is everything that one has assimilated and integrated. What has not been really integrated, really become you, becomes a block, becomes a fixed gestalt, which is in the way of the ongoing gestalt formation, and what is really the aim of any good therapy: the ongoing gestalt formation where whatever is of greatest interest to the organism, to the person, to a relationship, to a group, even to a nation, comes into the foreground and becomes gestalt, something that stands out from all the rest. In the foreground one can cope with it and work on it, with it, through it, so that it can be in one way or another disposed of, finished, so that the foreground then becomes free again for the next relevant gestalt. And that we have to do in the Gestalt therapy and in any good therapy is really to focus on the fixed gestalt and behavior and principles and ideas, and it's mostly all the things which we take for granted. It's what in psychoanalysis is called resistance, and it's not enough to explain the resistance, to interpret it, or to see it as a transference phenomenon; but it is something that has become automatic, it has become second nature, and all so-called resistances are originally acquired as assistance for something in some situation, in an early situation usually. And if it is useful at that time it tends to become automatic, you rely on it, and what is automatic you are not aware of anymore: "That's how I am; that's how I have always been; I can't do anything about it." And what we do in Gestalt therapy is to de-automatize the fixed behavior, the fixed muscular attitudes, the fixed ideas, principles, and ideals.

What's your interest right now?

NED: I was just caught by your eye. My interest was centered right there on your eyes.

LAURA: What do you see?

NED: What just flashed through was a *New York Times Magazine* article on the greater chiefs and one thing they talked about was the quality of their eyes and their clarity and that's just what flashed as I was looking at you.

LAURA: So you escape into some kind of literary comparison.

NED: Not escape, I've just been coming back to the clarity. (Sighs)

LAURA: What are you so intent on? (She echoes his Sigh)

NED: I'm aware that down in Southern California I don't have much contact with you and I was looking forward to — interestingly enough — to being here today.

LAURA: Now you are aware that the day before yesterday you were looking forward to something that will be. And what is right now?

NED: Wanting to get in touch with me first.

LAURA: What are you in touch with now?

NED: I felt a flash of anger, like you're interpreting me. And I want to be left alone, my first few days of being a grandfather and kind of enjoying it. That's really what I'm most in contact with at the moment, kind of special and fresh. Also aware that I've not made much contact with you.

LAURA: What are you doing right now?

NED: Playing with it.

LAURA: What is *it*?

NED: Contact with you.

LAURA: You know, if you really make contact, you don't say, "I am making contact with you." That is a technical term and when I talk about it I can talk about making contact; but I look at you, I'm talking to you, you are looking at me, or you are thinking of something else. (Long silence) And now? You have in your whole attitude and posture something challenging. Just exaggerate it.

NED: I'm sure I'm trying to grow taller.

LAURA: How does it feel? What do you say to me now?

NED: If you challenge me, I'll feel challenged. I don't feel challenged.

LAURA: OK. What are you enjoying right now?

NED: I'm enjoying your trying to find something to reach me and I really appreciate that. I'm not quite sure — part of me starts to want to respond.

LAURA: Part of you. On the one hand. And on the other?

NED: I'm not quite sure what I want to do.

LAURA: Can you make a dialogue between these two parts?

NED: I did have an anticipation of being quiet. You're not letting me be quiet! It was like my own rehearsal and so I feel on the one hand a bit trapped.

LAURA: You came with a kind of a fixed gestalt ...

NED: To let go. To let myself let go, but I essentially wanted to be quiet, like, experience more internally, and I'm very accustomed to being outward. I can be excited about wanting to be more in touch with you and our relating. I feel kind of open and pleasant really. I'm past now ... because I wanted to be quiet and you haven't let me. I could have told you to go to hell!

LAURA (to group): If anyone makes any observations which are pertinent to what's going on, please come out with it.

EVE: I don't know what's going on but I don't like it. I don't know what my expectation was — some kind of experiential group — but I'm sitting here getting angry about what you're doing or not doing but I'm not sure why. I don't know how long I can sit. I'm thinking: am I going to get bored or angry or what?

LAURA: You say you are possibly bored or angry or nearly so and at the same time you say it in a very quiet voice. Just do that intentionally.

EVE: You mean exaggerate my posture?

LAURA: Ya. This is the only movement you can make in that position?

EVE: I can't even make any movement in this position. (Laughter)

LAURA: But you did, you see; you were shrugging your shoulders, which is the onset of some movement and immediately you're giving up. From this position this is support for withdrawing, for keeping yourself to yourself, and squeezing on your diaphragm, so in that position one doesn't really have sufficient support for making contact. Support really starts, apart from the primary physiology of circulation and breathing and digestion, with posture and mobility. I would like to see how you walk and stand. (Eve walks) Can somebody imitate how she walks? OK, you describe it yourself.

EVE: I'm trying to walk differently than I think I usually walk, by keeping my chest up and not worrying about my posture that much but I've wanted to learn how to walk better.

LAURA: Actually what one does in walking is that one transports one's whole bulk from one place to another and the center of gravity is in the pelvis and that must go forward and the legs are really only catchers. If you start with stiff legs then you walk more or less like this and everything is back; you see, if you really stiffen your legs, it throws the pelvis back and then you have to hold yourself up from here, from the chest and shoulders. The support must come from the upper carriage and that gives you then enough space to breathe and it also supports your guts. When this is too far back then you literally spill your guts unless you stiffen your muscles. If the pelvis is under then the guts are supported, you *have* guts and the upper part of the body remains free for orientation and manipulation.

EVE: I always have the sense of being pulled down on this side, like a gravitation, though I try to fight against it.

LAURA: Just come a little bit further in. Ya, this is rather higher. Lie down on the floor on your back, knees up a bit, your stomach, and relax, and your head loose — there's a little tension there — and inhale against my hand. You see, you pull all the air up there. Actually, in the prone position, stomach breathing gets more into action if you don't prevent it. You automatically and habitually pull everything up here. Inhale against my hand and make that hole in the back bigger and exhale as if you were exhaling right here through the middle of the spine, not pushing but just letting the air flow out and let the spine glide against the floor ... And see what happens with the pelvis when the spine straightens more. You can practice this also against the wall or against the floor, and one doesn't have to be that straight all the time as when one is against the floor, but what I am really after is the mobility of the spine so that you can mobilize any sort of support that is necessary for whatever you are doing at the time. Just roll up with the head first ... stretch your legs and roll down again from here, lean everything forward and roll against the floor, and now the other way, put your legs over your head. You *can* do it, you see, you have the mobility here. Now go down slowly, one vertebra after another. Actually, all the vertebrae can be moved separately except the last three or four that are linked at the tail end. You have the mobility still so you can do it comparatively easy but of course in order to acquire a different habit one must first feel what one is actually doing and then you can experiment with doing something else. I was lucky I started that choral dancing when I was eight and then later did a lot of other choral dance and eurythmic work in the other German systems and once you have acquired that kind of support and mobility it really holds good all your life. I'm 75 and it's still there. I don't think I could do a lot of the work I am doing without it. So it's a very basic support: the breathing, the alignment, and the freedom of head and shoulders and arms. Are you aware that your left shoulder is much higher than the right?

EVE: Yes, I've overcompensated.

LAURA: Do you feel the tension?

EVE: No, I feel the pull of gravity on the other side, this side.

LAURA: Just come up again. (To another member) Put that away, it doesn't help taking notes. (Laughter) You are pushing and pulling, you see. You are very controlling. Do that intentionally. Do you feel that you pull your leg?

EVE: Not a lot.

LAURA: And most of the time you left your eyes on me and I felt as long as you do that you are looking in some way for I don't know what – approval? For approval that you are doing it right?

EVE: Probably.

LAURA: And to that extent you are not really in and with the movement but more on how it looks or how you look to me. Actually I don't criticize in that way that something is right or wrong or you should do it better. I take it the way it comes, the way you do it, and that's how it is at the moment and we start with that.

I would like to say a little more about support and contact. Contact is not something that one is in or out of but something one makes, one does; and one also does whatever is in the way of making contact. And the awareness of that is what we are supporting in Gestalt therapy, the awareness *how* you interfere with the free flow of awareness. (To another group member): You don't have to make notes. This is all in an article I published in *VOICES* in 1978.

(To Jan): You are thinking what?

JAN: At the moment I was just flexing my foot, this foot that's tired from wearing high-heeled shoes and tramping around Central Park. I was flexing my foot and it felt good.

LAURA: Can you walk in high heels?

JAN: Well, that's a good question. Mostly I've been doing that the last couple of hours. Can I? Well, I did.

LAURA: Just walk without them and then walk with them. Let's see what changes happen ... Ya, the spine is also pretty hollow.

JAN: I have a very severe back problem.

LAURA: Sure.

JAN: Sure what?

LAURA: When there is this habitual tension, then you have a back problem.

JAN: I don't know which came first. You obviously have your ideas on which came first.

LAURA: This tension in the back, which leads to the tension in the diaphragm and to a reduction of breathing, this is the most central way of exercising self-control.

JAN: I'm very into that, that's right.

LAURA: And of reducing your energy. It's not using the free space of your chest, your lungs.

JAN: I think that's probably true. I think I've done it for a long, long time. It is a well-established habit by now.

LAURA: I also notice that you let the air out and then you talk when you have almost nothing left and then your voice gets lower and lower.

JAN: I'm not aware of that.

LAURA: Do that intentionally.

JAN: See, I can talk with no air. It is very low.

LAURA: It is how you were talking just now.

JAN: And I was not aware of that. I can't stand still for very long, my back starts to hurt and I have to start moving.

LAURA: I'm pretty sure.

JAN: It doesn't surprise you.

LAURA: You could do a similar exercise on the floor.

JAN: I don't think I want to in this attire.

LAURA: You don't have to do it now and you don't get results from doing it once. This is something one really has to work on. You'll find if you have that kind of support that it increases your energy and you maintain it longer.

JAN: Are you talking about doing the same thing she did lying on the floor?

LAURA: Ya, starting to mobilize the middle of the spine more. See, a four-footer has it comparatively easy; immediately he stands on all fours and has support enough to walk immediately but the head is fixed between the shoulders and there is no manipulation at all and an ape may walk on his four limbs and grab something with his hind leg but it's only a human being that finally gets up on his hind leg and uses the undercarriage mainly or only for support and locomotion, and the upper part of the body for orientation and manipulation. And with better alignment and more mobility here and more support from your pelvis you get better functioning and more concentration also. Are you doing any sort of physical exercise at all?

JAN: I've just started seeing Ilana Rubenfeld for some Alexander work; I've just had one session. I'm going to see her three days this week and I'm doing some exercises. I see a chiropractor. I'm really trying to get well.

LAURA: And if you do any sort of dancing or gym, don't do ballet, because that emphasizes out-turned legs only and elevation. You get up this way, but you can't possibly from this position carry anything or do anything else. It's just for itself, like coloratura singing, that can also be very beautiful but it is also very limited in expression.

JAN: Would Yoga be good for it?

LAURA: Some of it. There are some overstretching things that I'm not very happy about. Also Bioenergetics, some of the exercises, the things are very usable in the frame of Gestalt but I think any strong manipulation I would reject because it tends to break through, to hit through a resistance without seeing that there is sufficient support when it's done, and I have seen psychotic breakdowns in certain borderline people with Bioenergetics, so I would be very careful there. Actually, nearly any technical modality is usable on appropriate occasions within the framework of Gestalt. Gestalt is really a philosophical aesthetic concept. In Germany an art school is called a Hochschule fur Gestaltung. Gestalt means figure, shape, form, a total thing that stands out from its ground and the relationship between the figure and its ground is what we call meaning because its support comes from what has become our background, what has become assimilated and integrated, and what has *not* been assimilated really, that means worked through, so that it can disappear like food that is well chewed, simply disappears, you don't have to swallow whole bits and pieces. If you do, you put a burden on the stomach, work that should be performed in the mouth. And the eating pattern is really direction giving for the way one goes about learning and making contact with the world at large, with the other. You see, the infant is originally in confluence with the mother. The embryo is part of the mother and gradually starts developing on its own, first with the heartbeat and movement, and then in birth with breathing, but the feeding still restores the original confluence. The child is really aware only when it's hungry and uncomfortable, but as soon as it has slept onto the breast or the bottle the tension is essentially reduced and the child can go to sleep again, and even go on feeding while it is asleep.

The child starts making contact with the other as the other when the teeth start shooting in and the gums harden and the hands are touching and you are aware of touching the other and then it depends on the feeding methods which are used whether the child develops a way of really taking time over what it is doing, what it is getting and chewing it through, or whether it is stuffed very quickly much too long with baby foods which are mushy, and swallows. Unfortunately, we are taught in school in a similar way. Everything is somehow prechewed and stuffed into kids in a half-digested way, and they shove it in before the exam and spout it out in the test and are rid of it forever after. I've never seen so many people as here in America where they go to school so long and do so much homework and in the end know so very little. You laugh, but it's really sad.

LIL: It's the way you put it, but the fact itself is not funny. There's a kind of irony, I think, in that statement, there is for me, and probably for most of us in this room when I think of how long I went to school.

LAURA: Ya, most of it you forget.

LIL: Oh yes, and a lot of it I didn't want to know in the first place.

LAURA: This way of swallowing uncritically really supports the confluence — originally with the mother, but then with the family, and with school and with sports, and with the political system — and whatever doesn't fit into the confluence tendency is alienated. It doesn't fit in and one feels guilty about it and also resentful. In every confluence relationship there is one who has the upper hand and the other one — like in the family or class or whatever — they follow, they fall in with the wishes and needs of the leader, father, teacher, president, the boss. I try to prevent that, right now, here: not simply to swallow what I say and take it at face value, but taste it and put your teeth into it. Actually, language has very precise words for that: one talks about putting one's teeth into something, chewing it through, assimilating it, biting off more than one can chew, being fed up to the back teeth.

MAC: That's about where I'm fed up to now.

LAURA: Right now?

MAC: Because I want you to stop talking, and at the same time I don't want to be on the spot and now I'm doing...

LAURA: Make a dialogue between these two parts.

MAC: No. I just want you to stop the talk and I don't want to do what you're going to tell me to.

LAURA: So what do you want?

MAC: I don't know.

PAT: He wants somebody else to do it.

MAC: Yeah. I want something to happen, that's right.

JOAN: And now it's not. I share your feelings. I'm sitting here just getting angrier and angrier but I don't want to go through that again. I just don't want to feel I've wasted my time here, and that's how I feel right now.

LAURA: I would like a little more feedback.

GERT: I feel nauseous but I'm taking it in and taking it in and I'm in conflict whether to stay or leave.

LAURA: This is of course always the trouble with a new group which isn't really a group but an assemblage of people that I don't really know whom I'm talking to. And so I'm necessarily talking at you. On the other hand, I feel, particularly in the last few years, that I have to be much more didactic than I used to be because people do something all the time and they want something to happen and to be excited and they don't know what they are doing.

JEAN: I really came here to experience you, which I'm doing, so I'm not crying bored or angry but I guess I'd like to experience you more in terms of how you work. I guess my own feeling anyway — I couldn't agree with you more, that probably 98% or 99.9%, everything I've learned I've forgotten and I guess that's how I always feel about theoretical stuff, that if something happens that makes it meaningful then it becomes part of me, and if not, then I could write it down but won't read my notes, or if I did I wouldn't remember it anyway, that doesn't sink in for me. That's for me.

LAURA: By itself it doesn't sink in, unless you...

JEAN: Unless I use it.

LAURA: Do something with it.

JEAN: Yes.

LAURA: Right now I notice that you pulled your elbows in and just shrugged, just with your hands. Just do that intentionally. Just do that and exaggerate it.... No, you are lifting more here. But when you were talking to me ... How does it look to you?

JEAN: When you did it, I wasn't really aware of my doing it. But when you did it, it looked to me like you were trying to say, "Well, it's not so important," like undercutting what I was saying.

LAURA: Also impeding your reach. Just moving from here and reducing your space.

GUS: I would very much appreciate your making a contract with somebody to do some work so everybody could watch.

LAURA: Well, what about you?

GUS: Fine.

LAURA: What do you want to work on?

GUS: In general I've been aware of my dreams and transformation that's taking place with me. I'm giving away clothes. I'm buying different kinds of clothes. I'm saying all kinds of things to me in my behavior. It's new. And I'm aware I'm looking away from you and grabbing some of the things that have happened in the last day or two that I haven't put together yet. I haven't really chewed on them and I'm mystified as to what I'm saying to me.

LAURA: Are you aware that after every sentence you either smile or bite your lip? Do that intentionally. Exaggerate it. How do you feel when you do it?

GUS: Like I'm clamping down. And to me, that's part of the issue. Much of me — I'm going into the past again but it's very familiar to what's happening with me now — in relationship to a significant other friend of mine. We're swapping roles. It's new to me. It's just within the last day and I'm getting used to a new assertiveness I've not had. I like it, but it's strange and a little scary. I'm strange. I'm a little scary. I'm aware that as I own it my jaws are a little looser. So I'm able to bring in air easier and give myself some energy.

LAURA: You also let it out and then talk with nothing. Would you just inhale and let your voice out on "AH" so that it hits me.

GUS: AHHH.

LAURA: You cut off. There's much more.

GUS: AHHHHHHHH. I'm aware that I stop...

LAURA: You push it out from here. Really fill yourself, let it come in and then let it out. And whatever you want to say right now, feel it however you can, like a recitative in an opera.

GUS: I think I could be Boris.

LAURA: Sing that.

GUS: Boris — how's that?

LAURA: Sing that.

GUS: BORIS ...

LAURA: You see, when it's all out, you start talking. The voice carries on the exhalation. That's why singing is such a good exercise for people who don't let out their voice, don't use it. Then you get into this kind of indefinite thing, generalizing, making up in quantity what you don't get across in quality. Quality comes through letting the energy go through.

GUS: I'm aware of breathing deeper and my asshole is unwinding. I'm aware of sweating a little right now, perspiring.

LAURA: You let it out everywhere else except the voice. (Group laughter)

GUS: That brings a flood of past associations, because I've been accused of being too forceful.

LAURA: Be too forceful right now, or what you think is too forceful. Get up and throw your weight around.

GUS: Laura, I wish you'd do something for us. We've been sitting here like bumps on a log.

LAURA: Speak for yourself.

GUS: I've been sitting here like a bump on a log. I've been aware of Hall falling asleep and I've been aware of my own falling asleep and I agree with what's been said. We've been talking too much and not doing enough and I feel much better now that I'm talking and doing something. Now that I'm doing it, it doesn't sound all that forceful.

LAURA: And again you smile at the end of every sentence, as if...

GUS: Yeah. "Don't hit me, I'm smiling you know." It's almost ... I expect to be punished for being too forceful. Yeah. That goes way back.

LAURA: Well, just look around. Who would punish you here? Tell us.

GUS: Well, I don't think anybody would. No, I don't think you would. In fact I'm kind of experiencing in me the amusement I see in your eyes. That I may need protection, but ... (Laughter) I can be forceful, at least in this, the way I feel now, and not ...

LAURA: Be forceful with your left hand. Ya, see, you leave the right hand free and you put the left away.

GUS: I've introjected an awful lot of not being forceful. I might override people and I never thought I would have felt that powerful in the first place, but I've gotten a lot of feedback that I am and it never quite jibed.

LAURA: You are telling us stories which we can believe or not believe.

GUS: Well, I thought it was interesting.

LAURA: Say something to a few people here, that's either critical or that you think ordinarily you wouldn't say. Try now with me.

GUS: You are not as painted by the people I know in Cleveland and I'm both delighted and intrigued. I don't think I would have said that before.

DAVE: Would you translate that? What's painted?

GUS: With word pictures. Laura has been painted to me and to others who were trained in Cleveland by the Cleveland Gestalt Institute — and I think the world of these people there because I've learned a great deal from them and grown because of their influence so that for me this is a way of connecting.

LAURA: How?

GUS: How am I doing that? I'm not aware.

LAURA: Well, I don't know to whom you talked in Cleveland but they have learned a lot from me. I think what most of you are not aware of yet is that observation that I am coping with very small things and making small steps is and can be very exciting, and that is really where most of the difficulties are embedded. I do minute work which is not perhaps immediately visible or understandable. I observe and deal with small things or what is usually taken for granted, what is called obvious because it is in the obvious that resistances and difficulties are embedded. The word obvious and the word problem, they are linguistically actually the same. *Problema* means in Greek what is right before you, and obvious is the same as right here in your way and we use the one for what is too trivial even to think about it, let alone to talk about it and we use the word problem for what's difficult and one has to work through or one has to get around or one has to get it behind one.

CHRIS: So are you saying that if someone comes to you to therapy with a problem that has to do with somebody outside, a spouse or a child or a boss or something...

LAURA: If he has the problem outside it is right here with me and I can see it and I find that if you really observe you can find it right here now but if you – that in working with somebody just on the most obvious thing it can immediately be demonstrated and experimented with, that that leads directly to a central conflict.

TOM: Do you still want some feedback about what we were experiencing as you were working, or would you rather work with the people as you are now?

LAURA: You say there is something that you want to say.

TOM: I have different feedback from the rest of them. The expression that comes to my mind at this moment is "to take pride." I was taking pride in the work that you were doing. So much of what I know about Gestalt I was observing you doing as it was taking place and I was watching people and I was observing eyes drifting off and people restless and I was wondering if somehow we were missing the Gestalt concepts that I was experiencing, maybe they would call it minutiae but I'm aware of the difference between foreground and the work that has to be done and the people who come to me for work don't need me to tell them the obvious and what they know. They need me to help them focus in on what they don't see and that's what I saw you doing. And even when you lectured I could tune in to the Gestalt concepts. What I experienced in terms of what maybe was happening to the group — maybe I'm projecting, but I've worked with both you and Fritz so I don't really know, but if you think so I'm more than willing to do that kind of work with you in the here and now — is that you work differently than Fritz does.

LAURA: Certainly.

TOM: But you're a different kind of human being. This is what I teach my supervisees. I think I have a sense of people expecting a second-hand Fritz to come in and sit down and say, "Here's the hot seat, who wants to work? Fuck you, you don't want to work? Somebody else take the hot seat." And that's not the way you work.

LAURA: No, I would work with someone for quite a while, and if people really pay attention they get something from that.

TOM: I think they were looking for something gigantically exciting and I think that's a part of the difficulty with our here-and-now generation.

BESS: I think you're making an assumption.

TOM: That's what Fritz would tell us — that 99% of what we see is projection, so you learn of another gestalt. I don't know, I may be projecting but I experience Laura's work very differently. That's all I'm saying.

NAN: What I hear you saying is, "Is that all there is?"

JILL: I didn't see the statements being made as necessarily about Laura's work, but statements about a lot of where each of us were.

NAN: Which statements are you talking about?

JILL: Some of the statements. It wasn't about Laura but about where each of us were. For me, I had low energy. In some ways I was wishing something would happen because I have real low energy and was real tired.

LAURA: Ya, you were not aware of what was happening.

JILL: Well, I was aware of what was happening. I was also aware that there were people who were feeling they wanted something else to happen and I didn't hear all of that as a negation of you. I heard you defending her in some way and I didn't hear her being negative.

LAURA: I'm used to these kinds of reactions in the first hour of work — and I reject the encounter techniques. Gestalt therapy is not an encounter therapy, with getting at set exercises and challenges and do's and don't's.

TOM: I'm aware at this moment that I've allowed myself to be vulnerable by what I've said and I have to put myself on the railroad tracks and the train can come down and I'm the asshole that put myself there. But I just felt the need to say it not so much for the rest of the people here but for somebody that I brought here to be with you today and we traveled a long distance to come here. Maybe I was defining you from her. I'm not sure. It's possible, but I do know that you do work differently from Fritz.

LAURA: Do you feel I needed it or she needed it?

TOM: I feel I needed it. I was being paradigmatic when I was showing them how powerful you were.

LAURA: That reminds me of an experience that I had several years ago when I was at Martin Buber's 80th birthday party, and Erich Fromm was giving an address and in the course of the address he said something, "Power is what makes machines and animals out of people," and I felt he really was not giving himself credit as a therapist and I wanted to say something at the end, and then Buber got up first, of course, and thanked him for the address and said, "But in one respect I don't agree with you. Power is not this or this, but it is ... (She probably does some nonverbal gesture here).

I pay so much attention to support functions because if the boundary experience is disturbed by insufficient support, then the boundary, the discrimination between what is me and what is the other, becomes blurred and malfunctions and that opens the door to projection and introjection so these are not really the primary things to cope with — you can talk about it until you are blue in the face — but you really have to strengthen the support functions.

RUTH: I'm thinking of asking you to help me with something, and I'm split because my thought before was, I don't like the sort of voting that splits us up and I would feel more comfortable if there were a way to...it feels like something isn't being told in the group or there's some kind of restlessness and I was aware of it before when I was standing up. I would feel more comfortable to do something myself or to see somebody else if somehow it felt better on the whole. I feel my attention very scattered; it keeps jumping around — to you, to myself, to the discontent. I think we could get so I could at least feel a little more comfortable if everybody were less scattered and so I'm betwixt and between myself and sensing what's going on and wishing we could all change it, not just you, and it feels like there's enough bad vibes in this room and snarling looks and frowny faces and people raising their eyes to heaven and snorting around and it stinks and I don't think we ought to do this together. I wish we could all do something a little better together. We should be able to do something more than what we are; it shouldn't just be up to you.

LAURA: That's right.

EVE: I don't have that feeling because I came to experience Laura Perls, as a famous person, as an expert, whatever. I really didn't know what to expect. And also came on lots of people's recommendations and as I said before, I don't think anything's been happening here. I mean there are some of us — me — I've had some experience with Gestalt work, I see what you're doing, and you're not doing anything that makes me feel I'm learning anything, I'm hearing anything different, I'm experiencing anything, and I'm still sitting here ...

LAURA: Then you forget already what you did here?

EVE: That's nothing. I didn't do anything here. I'm sorry. I've been working on this, I've got a pelvic tilt. I also had an opportunity to work with Feldenkrais. I've not integrated it and I've not really put it together because I've had to deal with another problem. That's nothing. I don't consider that...that's not work. That's not really dealing with my posture.

BESS: But do you expect her to do it all?

EVE: I don't expect her to do anything. Not to do it all or to do a specific thing. It was written up that this would be an experiential group and I've been to other experiential workshops and had very good experiences and I'm not having one now. And I don't think what I did up there — that's silly — that's a waste of time for me, as far as I'm concerned. Besides, I do the pelvic tilt at home. I exercise. I didn't really think that was going anywhere. When she goes around and says, "Do it deliberately" — if I hear that one more time I think I'll bust.

LAURA: Would you like to take over the group?

EVE: No.

JILL: I'd really like to see us deal with the experience we're having right now because that might be the best experience we could have.

JAN: I'm experiencing a lot of nervousness right now. I'm sort of torn, like I didn't want to say anything and now, I'm gonna say it. I hear what you're saying and I'm sorry you didn't get anything out of your experience. I certainly did, and I feel sorry that you didn't because I did so much. And I've been appreciating a lot of your work and some other people's work. I appreciated your working with standing up and I feel, I was feeling a little excited about what's happening here and I felt when you said about people being discontented, I guess I'm not aware of that. It wasn't in my foreground. I was really quite taken with what I was hearing and, I mean, I've heard it before, somehow it goes in differently and I'm experiencing a lot more pleasure, so, anyway ...

GREG: Eve, I'm wondering if what you do here is a real option for you. I say that because, you know, primarily I hear you blaming. Sometimes when I feel that way and I don't feel like moving anything forward and I feel some internal distress, I tend to walk out, you know, rather than blame. I don't want to get involved. I'm not encouraging that, but I'm wondering if you feel somehow trapped by visions of power or whatever. This is a hotel room where you can do anything you want. I was wondering, if you take yourself seriously, then why stay? If it turns out, God forbid, that Laura Perls happens to be a person, and isn't a goddess, and that's a disappointment to us, then why blame her, or why blame the group?

EVE: You're doing an awful lot of interpreting and projecting and I don't want to respond to that.

MEG: I have a strong reaction. I don't want us to spend our time with people in the group talking to other people in the room, not that people might not say good or bad things but because we've all been to millions of groups, I'm sure, and I really came to hear you and I'm having, first of all, I think you're incredibly sharp and I'm feeling very jealous. My other reaction is: My God! 75! So I don't have to give up when I hit 70, and that's very inspiring and I feel very inspired by it. I didn't know what you looked like, and when I saw you I thought, "That's Laura?" Like, "old lady" — so that's very inspiring too.

LAURA: I feel I'm getting older by the minute.

MEG: The other thing I'm feeling inspired by and jealous of is, I was thinking, "Oh my God, if I were leading a group and people said this to me, *I* would walk out. And you're just sitting there calmly, saying, "Oh?" and I was thinking, "I'd be shaking," but you don't even look like you're shaking.

LAURA: Well, I'm not shaking.

MEG: I was feeling both admiring and jealous too.

CLARK: I experienced you as doing more than just sitting there and saying nothing. I turned around for the first time in my life and checked out my perception. I experienced her as constantly, no matter what you were saying, getting you to focus on you in terms of what you were saying about her and what you were experiencing as you were saying it and what your body was doing when you were saying it, over and over again, especially the work that she did with you. I thought that was a marvelous example of the Gestalt techniques that I've learned and that I've used. That's what I mean. I have a sense of so many of you, not all of you obviously, having missed what really went on. I don't know why that happened. I wish I did, so I would get better for my own workshops.

ELLA: I'm having so much trouble with this disharmony, as if it's my family and I've got to get the group together and why is it my job and it isn't and I'm self-appointed, so unhappy with it. Yuck! I want you all to be all nice so that everybody could get what they wanted and it's just like, oh no, we're mired down, some people don't want us to talk to each other, and some people don't want you to lecture and some people don't think anything is happening and other people think a whole lot is happening .... oooh!

LAURA: Coming with certain expectations in a certain direction, they will always be disappointed. That's how one prevents oneself from experiencing what is actually going on.

ELLA: I have the illusion that if you or we, if somebody could get a consensus, or if we could all agree. We never found out what all our expectations were. I came late so I think maybe you did that before I got here and I missed that part. So that we'd know what your design or thoughts or your — maybe you didn't have any and that's the grand scheme, and so we're doing what we're supposed to be doing. But it does feel as if we've got a lot of different agendas and we just keep knocking heads and it doesn't feel as productive to me either as it could.

KENT: Maybe we each create our reality in some crazy way. Maybe Laura's got one reality and each of us has some of our own.

ELLA: I would like to check out one thing. Was learning about what you do, in terms of holding back your aggression, or assertiveness, sufficient, or would you have needed or wished to have had help in having a corrective experience? I'd just like to know your experience.

GUS: I got in touch with a lot of things. I hesitate to go into "what if's."

ELLA: Do you feel a lack of being helped to experience?

LAURA: If you had wanted to, I would have gone on. At this point I wasn't pushing him. I don't know him very well. I can be very persistent.

GUS: I appreciated what you did, because I'm at a stage in my life where I don't want to have a corrective experience with somebody I don't know.

HAL: I want to share with you a supervisory statement that Fritz made to me about 12-13 years ago. We were discussing a case and he said to me, "Hal, Hal, you can't push." I'll never forget that. All you have to do is be with the patient where they are, that's all you have to do, be with them whatever.

LAURA: And see what they are doing or not doing. They are always doing something.

ANN: I used to always have something to work on and I realize I wasn't really feeling the need to say anything. I couldn't figure out why and then I realized I have been very touched by watching and I feel very moved and I don't have many words for it.

LAURA: You wanted to work on something before? You came with an idea?

ANN: It's a past thing for me, not a very current thing.

LAURA: So who does want to work?

LIZ: I'll work. Which shocked me 'cause I came here thinking, "I'm not going to work. I don't want to deal with it." I was thinking about it already. I don't know how to say it in a Gestalt way.

LAURA: There's a Gestalt way?

LIZ: This weekend I've been holding on to anger with my husband about something that I think I've made into a tremendous thing. It's not that it's nothing, which is what's unusual in our relationship, but I've really been very angry and trying to be angrier than I am trying to not talk with him at all, to act very angry and be hostile — and I think act angrier and I am, making a mountain out of a molehill — not a molehill but it's not a huge thing but I am aware of wanting a mountain out of it.

LAURA: Why do you have to do that?

LIZ: That's what I don't know. That's what I want to work on. It's not usually my style, so that it's not at all clear to me why I want to do that. I could tell you what it is.

LAURA: Do you feel he doesn't react otherwise?

LIZ: No, I can't say that. He's usually a pretty sensitive guy.

LAURA: Can you make a dialogue right now with him? Talk with him about this.

LIZ: "Look, I'm really sick and tired of when we get angry, that I kind of start the overtures of, 'Let's talk about it, let's understand what's going on.' Well you will, but I haven't talked to you since...what, Friday? Thursday night? This is Sunday? How long are you gonna wait? I know eventually you will; I'm not gonna move out. You'll eventually come out. Why should I have to go through all this? And the longer you don't talk to me, the angrier I get, you know that."

LAURA: What is he saying?

LIZ: What is he saying? He's saying, "I've been acting friendly. If you would talk to me, I would talk to you. I tried to discuss everyday life with you and you won't talk to me so why should I make myself vulnerable? Why should I make myself vulnerable to you when you're so angry? Nothing's such a big thing that you have to be so angry about it. I mean, if you're angry then you talk to me. I don't want to make myself vulnerable. And besides, I think I'm right. I think I'm right and I don't want to say I'm wrong when I think I'm right." That is what he'd say.

LAURA: With whom did you have to do that when you were a child? Shut up and not say anything?

LIZ: Who did *I* have to do that with? My mother always told me I never shut up. My mother. My mother always thinks she's right Either you don't mention it or you agree with her or you have a big fight or you walk out and you say, "All right, Mom, it's all right." I mean to this day she always thinks she's right.

LAURA: And you change your key. That's something that I noticed immediately that you spread frequently, "That's right, OK."

LIZ: Kind of like angry and attracted at the same time.

LAURA: Like showing your teeth.

LIZ: People tell me I'm a lot like my mother. (Laughter)

LAURA: This is what always happens. Children imitate with awareness what they admire and want to be like; and they identify unawares with what they can't stomach in any other way. And that way they avoid the outside conflict and they set up an inner one.

LIZ: I'm feeling that I'm very pulled in. I guess I'm feeling that I really would like to punch my husband now and I know it has nothing to do with him.

LAURA: I wish you would make a dialogue with your mother and tell her.

LIZ: Tell my mother? I was about to say "what?" "You know, Mom, I'm really sick and tired of your always having to be right. I'm also sick and tired of every time I tell you that, or try to talk to you or try to share what I feel about what goes on between us, that you kind of either get hurt, or you get this, 'Oh my God, Liz, I always have to walk on eggshells with you. Can't I just tell you what I feel? If I tell you what I feel? If I tell you what I feel or what I think, then you get all upset. What is this? You're a grown woman. I should be able to talk to you, you know. If I don't agree with you, then you get all upset.'" That's my mother. And I would say back the same thing to her, right? "That's not it, mother. If I don't agree with *you*, you get all upset. You know, your idea of being understanding and empathetic is to go through all the motions of being understanding and empathetic, but it's not really understanding. It's really kind of coping with, putting up with, loving, but it's not really understanding. It's not really trying to understand what I'm feeling. I feel you always come out of a defensive position, even though you don't seem defensive."

LAURA: I see you are both reproaching each other and in that way trying somehow to restore the original confluence to be in one camp or in the other. You want her to be more like you and she wants you to be more like her and to agree and none really acknowledges the other one as the other one. Could you say right now how you are different from your mother?

LIZ: "I guess I'm different in that I have a life in which I'm willing to take more risks than you are, and maybe

I'm not different underneath in being more rebellious, but I think I've given myself permission to do what I want to do. I think that you really chose to lead a life of conformity and that we're very different in this way, and I know it bothers you that my life doesn't conform to what you would consider to be the perfect life, and it bothers me that it bothers you that I live my life the way I do and that my sisters and my brother live their lives the way they do. It bothers me most of all that you're so upset about it, and that you feel like such a failure. Where did you go wrong? All your friends' children married well-to-do men or women who are Jewish and live in the suburbs and have three kids. I'd just like to live with your disapproval. It's harder to live with your feeling so really hurt and disappointed in yourself. I guess I keep wanting somehow either to make it up to you, though I'm not willing to do that at my own expense, or at least to get so angry at you. Can't you see that things are all right? You're making yourself miserable for nothing."

LAURA: You see, that's really her responsibility. And you're making yourself miserable over that — that's *your* responsibility.

LIZ: The point is, it's like I know that I'm making myself miserable over this thing with my husband.

LAURA: There is the same thing, that you don't fully acknowledge the difference, and let him be. I think that he lets you be much more than you let him be.

LIZ: That's true. That's definitely true. I'm spoiled, I'm so used to his letting me be that it's precisely about something that he wasn't letting me be about that I said, "He's not letting me be. How can he do that to me?"

LAURA: You want him to be mother?

LIZ: I want him to be the good mother, sure. Most of the time he does pretty good. Maybe that's the other side of it. I'm very aware of the part — I have a two-year-old and I'm pregnant and part of really what I've been feeling is, "How can he treat me that way when I'm pregnant?" Now I'm aware that I need special consideration, not that there's anything specially wrong, but I need special consideration and he shouldn't put more demands on me.

LAURA: Actually, you are continually playing mother with yourself, by aggravating yourself, and at the same time holding, so that you play both parts. What we are trying right here and now is to externalize the conflict again and see what is you and what is her.

LIZ: I want to say something about the content of our fight because it may be relevant too, which is that I have a friend who is bisexual but most of whose affairs are with women, and I arranged to have dinner with her and I mentioned it Thursday night when I came home: "By the way, I'm having dinner with this friend." And he got this real attitude: "How come you have to see her every so often?" That's like about four times a year. "How come you have to see her? Why do you have this compulsion?" He didn't say that but that was the indication, and then he got into all this thing about why she would want to see me but I know that's not true. If I were having supper with a straight friend he would say "Oh," or whatever. He wouldn't mind, he's not like that, but he and I knew that he was threatened. I have other gay friends and stuff and I knew that he was threatened by the idea that maybe I'm gay. And uh...

LAURA: What does it mean to you?

LIZ: Well, that's what I'm asking myself too, because why should that upset me so much? Because it's very much in contrast, you know, I mean I feel like first of all if I were gay I'd be gay; it wouldn't be like the end of the world. And if I were bisexual, I'd be bisexual. That's all on an intellectual level and I don't feel like...

LAURA: How do you feel?

LIZ: You're asking me how. I'm avoiding it. I think I feel very mixed. I guess just as there's a part of me that's glad I'm white — that's a terrible thing to say, right? — I guess there's a part of me that's glad I'm straight. And ... 'cause I know what I kept saying to myself is, "Shit! Now come on, I'm raising his child and I'm pregnant. I'm going to have another child and all that the idiot could come out with is: He doesn't know I'm straight." If your own husband doesn't know you're straight, who's gonna know you're straight? Like, I mean, but it wasn't really on a real level. I wasn't really taking it as an insult about my sexuality, but I was wondering why this should upset me so much. That's why I thought I should bring it up.

LAURA: Any comments?

EVE: I don't think that its coming up at this time and also coming up with your feelings about your mother is unrelated to your being pregnant and being connected for a time to a child.

LIZ: I was feeling that very strongly but it had a strong feeling connection to me of, "How can he say that to me when I'm pregnant?"

LAURA: Make a few generalizations about gay people.

LIZ: Well I guess I'll just say what comes to mind even though I'm not proud of them. I'm feeling like this really goes against all my beliefs. OK. Gay women. Gay women don't like men. I don't believe it but I'll say it anyway. Somehow the strongest thing that came to my mind is that gay women are choosing to live their lives without men.

LAURA: Are you aware that you are saying all that without any energy?

LIZ: Maybe I was saying that without energy, but I was feeling something kind of deep when I said that because something kind of came together for me that what being pregnant means to me is that it means to be tremendously dependent on my husband. I mean he does about 40-60 of child raising. I work, and he's home when I work, and I'm home when he works, and we don't see each other very much and it's the idea of having another child. It's also him too, and now it's going to be more of giving of ourselves and taking away of ourselves and my being much more dependent on him and especially the first year. I mean, really, I don't know how people raise children by themselves. I really don't know. And I guess

I was feeling at this time that "I'm making myself so vulnerable to you, how could you say that to me?" Really, 'cause there's no way that I would have chosen to have a child on my own without his support at any time. Certainly not having one and knowing what I'm letting myself in for, would I choose to do another one.

LAURA: What are you letting yourself in for?

LIZ: Not sleeping at night, not ever being able to go to the bathroom by yourself, never having any time to do anything when you have any energy, not having time to read, not having time to be a person except to go to work and being a person with your children.

LAURA: It would be so much easier to be gay.

LIZ: Yes, it would be a whole lot easier.

JAY: You might not even be pregnant.

LIZ: Well, we planned this child. Maybe that's why I want to be angry with him. Maybe there's a part of me that says I don't have to deal with this if I'm not talking to him. He'll go to bed, I'll stay up and read and go through my mail. I can't do too much, but in some ways it's like having stolen some time for myself if I'm not talking to him. At least the time I would spend with him right now I could have to myself.

LAURA: Did you want this second child or is it an accident?

LIZ: No, we planned this child. And I'm very excited about it too. There's the side of it too, but you know, we have a two-year-old. It's the memory of what the early part of it is like, it's not very far away. And two is twice the work of one.

I'm feeling a hundred percent better. I'm feeling I can go home and talk to him. Of course he doesn't know where I am today. I said, I'm not going to call him and tell him where I'm going. He probably went home and thought, "I'll have some peace and quiet for a change."

SAM: Have the two of you talked about it a lot about having one more child?

LIZ: Why did you ask that?

SAM: I asked it because I wondered if that's one of the reasons about him not talking to you now. I kept hearing the word "support" — support — support.

LIZ: I guess what you're picking up is that probably we both feel that we're operating at maximum now, between really trying to be there for our daughter and really trying to be there for each other and also working and leading our lives that it doesn't feel that there's a whole lot left over and if you're going to have another child and give a whole lot more, then you have to wonder how much we're going to have left over for each other. I think we're both feeling that, so that maybe we're both feeling in need of love.

LAURA: You talk about energy and possibly not having enough and at the same time the way you hold yourself is really a way of depriving yourself. You talk about having to do things at the same time — you know, when

I sit like that I feel more like withdrawing, not doing anything. (Apparently she does a bit of work with how Liz is sitting)

ANN: I want to take back what I said about there not being anything to work on. I would like to explore what happened to me. I told you I was touched and you looked back at me and I let you touch something inside me. I think I know what it's about but I'm not sure. I'm living in a new town and I'm 50 miles away from my friends and I'm working in a hospital primarily with people who are terminally ill and it is very touching to work with them but they do not let me touch them very much. Physically, they will let me hold their hand but they have a lot of distance. And I feel like I come away with a gap most of the time. And I guess I don't know what to do about that. I don't know how to reach one or if I can't do that, if I should just say, well...

LAURA: For whom do you have to do that, or want to do that for?

ANN: I'm not sure. That feels confusing because I don't have my supports. My support people are not with me any more, so I have all new people and I want somebody to touch me and I want to touch them and the flow's not there in this new place, and I feel very unsure about what to do about that. I have felt myself being very reluctant...

LAURA: Do you make other contacts, apart from the hospital?

ANN: I've been there two months and...

LAURA: The people in the hospital, they are dying and they don't care so much. They can't give you very much except perhaps a certain example of how one faces it.

ANN: They don't want much from me. I think that's the other part of it.

LAURA: You want to be needed.

ANN: I think so. I hadn't thought of that before but now that occurs to me. I don't think they need very much.

LAURA: Who needs you most right now?

ANN: I don't have somebody who needs me. I don't have somebody outside me who needs me right now.

LAURA: It's a difficult thing, you know. It's something you want but it's not something you absolutely need. A child needs it, growing kids need it, one needs it at certain moments of one's life.

ANN: I think when everything changes for me the way it's done recently I once again feel like I need it because I hadn't much of that as a child, so I feel needy about it again. But it's good to be reminded that I don't need it like I once did.

LAURA: Perhaps you were also told, you don't need it, you have everything? Something like that?

ANN: Not in so many words, but yes.

LAURA: Start a whole row of sentences with, "I want."

LAURA: Start a whole row of sentences with, "I want."

ANN: What I was first aware of was that I wanted contact with you. I want to look at you. I wanted you to look at me. I want to talk to you. I want you to hear me out, to hear you.

LAURA: Do you need your glasses all the time?

ANN: Pretty much, I can't see..

LAURA: Take them off.

ANN: Take them off? OK. I know you're there but I can't see your face.

LAURA: What do you have to do now in order to see me again?

ANN: Oh. Come closer. OK. Now I can see you.

LAURA: Leave your glasses off whenever you don't absolutely need them. You see, you grab with your eyes. That lengthens the eye muscles and you get more and more short-sighted. Close your eyes. Relax. Try to get the feeling that your eyes are falling back into your head. How are you breathing?

ANN: A little bit shallow.

LAURA: Ya. When you open your eyes, open them softly and let come in whatever comes in. Don't grab for it. Whatever you see. Close them again. Feel any tension anywhere?

ANN: A little here and a little here.

LAURA: If you would exaggerate that, emphasize the tension around your eyes and your cheeks, your mouth, ya! How does that feel?

ANN: It feels like crying of some kind. A little crying ...

LAURA: What didn't you let yourself cry about?

ANN: What do I let myself cry about?

LAURA: *Don't* let yourself cry about.

ANN: Now? When I was little or when I was grown up? When I was little? How unhappy I was, then. That's what I didn't cry about when I was little. And I did not grieve when I lost people.

LAURA: Well, Freud said that already, that one has to do the mourning labor, and that goes with crying. And one cries about loss, or not getting or not having what one wants or what one needs. That's why infants cry such a lot because they can't do anything else about it, whatever they need. Grown ups cry when they lose somebody or something or a relationship. Who do you think of?

ANN: I think of two or three of my friends whom I left that I miss a whole lot.

LAURA: Talk to one of your friends right now. Tell them how you feel.

ANN: I miss you ... so much (tears). Sometimes I don't have anybody to talk to about things that matter ... I don't have a shoulder to cry on — yet. I don't have anybody who puts their arms around me — yet ... (long tearful silence). I think it feels like if I cry I'll quit missing them and I really don't want to quit missing them 'cause I don't want to give them up completely (Much fuller crying). When I cry, I cry out of my skin. It's not just out of my eyes.

LAURA: How do you feel now? Listen to your voice.

ANN: Better. Not so tired.

LAURA (to group): Any questions? Any comments? Who wants to work with a dream?

MARA: It's a recurring dream about being in a room.

LAURA: Say it in the present, "I am ... "

MARA: I am in a room, and there's all my papers and magazines and they're suffocating me, and, but I'm afraid that without them I'll die or there won't be any tomorrow and I don't know how to stop being suffocated or how to get out from under or what to do about the papers and the books and there seem to be more books and papers.

LAURA: Identify with the papers.

MARA: "Well, I'm the papers that you may need to teach this course again. I'm the papers that you may need to write a book. I'm the papers that you may need to give to patients to read. And you really can't get rid of me."

LAURA: What are you saying?

MARA: That I'm stuck, that part of me wants to get out from under, and yet part of me is really scared.

LAURA: Make a dialogue between these two parts.

MARA: I would like to be free. I would like to start over anew, fresh. I would like to have a clean room and a clean office.

(AS PAPERS): You can't do without me. You'll never know if you'll need me again. Or you will always need to have something to do in the future, so that you'll know you'll survive. You need to have me there with you.

(AS SELF): I really don't need these papers. I'm scared, but I'd like to free myself so I can be more creative, free from these papers and from these past experiences.

LAURA: You find that you are suffocating under that...

MARA: Yes, under the pile.

LAURA: So what do you need more?

MARA: Free space...air...

LAURA: Are you breathing right now?

MARA: Not well (takes deep breath). I just don't give myself the space.

LAURA: Ya, you're half suffocating yourself all the time.

MARA: Part of me feels protected by the papers and the other part of me feels suffocated.

LAURA: What do they protect, your papers?

MARA: They really ... I have my little animals that I take with me each time that I go to the hospital and then I survive. And it's like, if there's papers around they're an indication that I'll be back tomorrow. I haven't settled on staying alive. I know I'm going to, but I haven't settled on it. The papers are an indication that I exist and will exist.

LAURA: Just imagine there was a fire and the papers were burned. (Mara doesn't follow up on this.) If you could change the dream, how would you change it?

MARA: The dream is also reality. How would I change it? Boxes of material and to have to read everything, for which I certainly don't have time and never will. That somehow, if I'm existing or surviving or working without them, then somehow, though I get anxious even thinking about just checking the box, I can possibly do it. I don't know. It's really scary.

LAURA: And now you are looking at it, really, for the first time. All these papers protect you against people.

MARA: Against people?

LAURA: Papers you can read, you can occupy your time. You can surround yourself with it, build a wall of papers.

MARA: But I don't really do that. They're like having sleeping pills in the medicine cabinet without ever taking them.

LAURA: Ah! You just have it in case ...

MARA: In case. Yeah.

LAURA: Security at any price, if you took sick.

MARA: I don't know. I know I made a move and I got a good medical report, so I wiped that connection out. And I certainly don't sit with the papers. I basically am with people most of the time. One of my decisions is that writing is a lonely occupation and I don't do that.

LAURA: You are a room full of papers. I identify with that.

MARA: I am a room full of papers? God! I'm ugly and messy and most people are not too crazy about walking into that room. And it upsets my husband a great deal. And it also upsets me but I feel trapped.

LAURA: You *are* it.

MARA: I am the room with the papers?

LAURA: What are you doing right now?

MARA: Well, I'm trying to get rid of the notion that there's a mysterious something inside me which will grow and kill me one day. I know that that's not really true 'cause I've had good medical observations and I've also learned the Simonton technique but what scares me is that I won't do the technique well enough to survive. I won't do it right, and I even did it with them in that way. I made my drawings and then got scared about them and crossed them out – that I won't have the right imagery to work well and that's probably what's stopping me from getting rid of these papers.

LAURA: You try to live up to the image you have of yourself, to be right and doing things just so.

MARA: No, I just want to stay alive.

LAURA: Forever?

MARA: No, for a certain length of time, and I gave the responsibility to medicine and people are telling me I really have to take it on myself and I have to be — you know, this holistic medicine and stuff — I have to be responsible for myself. And that's very scary. I know I can do both. I also know that if the imagery doesn't work, there's always a doctor.

LAURA: Ya, and one doesn't stay alive but working at staying alive.

MARA: I know that.

LAURA: You stay alive through making alive contact. One is nourished through contact with the other, just like food that you assimilate becomes you.

MARA: I have a lot of that. I certainly have plenty of support and loving people but I've also been in the hospital a lot too and the papers, somehow this fake security blanket ...

LAURA: What's going on right now?

MARA: I'm wondering what's going to give me the peace of mind to clean up. To do it freely and feel OK about it.

LAURA: What do you feel right now?

MARA: I still am feeling a little bit scared.

LAURA: You're breathing rather shallowly again.

MARA: I keep seeing that room and wondering when I'm going to approach it and what am I going to do with it when I do.

LAURA: You are continually ruminating and worrying about what you are *going* to do and what's *going* to happen and in that way possibly missing out on what's available at the present time.

MARA: Except that this time I was much better. I was less anxious about seeing the surgeon.

LAURA: Back yourself up. Most people think always only of their front, that they have to present a good front, that they must be right. But it's the back, really, that gives you support and makes it possible to get the breathing support. Backbone and guts — that's really what's called courage. This is why I'm so keen on this coordination and alignment, because you certainly feel different when you are straight in your back and have room to breathe and you can hold yourself together. Don't think of yourself as just being up here (Laura points to head here), and that you have a body, but *be* a body. The

English language says very well, "When you *are* a body, you are *somebody*."

MARA: I gave my body to the doctors and I'm just reclaiming it. I'm just taking it back.

LAURA: Any questions?

DAN: I have one. I became aware that with a number of people who were working, there were hand gestures, things that they did with their hands, that were in the background and seemed to me to be part of the gestalt of what was going on. And I'm sure you were aware of them too. And I'd love to know, for you, why do you choose what you choose in terms of what you bring from the background into the foreground? I work so much more with the body in terms of: "Look at what you're doing now, don't change it, and what might it be saying?" etc., and I was contemplating as you were doing it whether you were dealing with what was being said rather than what the background was bringing up. I'd like to know where you were with that.

LAURA: I deal with what I feel is the easiest to deal with. I had the impression here, and particularly with her before, that dealing simply with the way she was holding herself or the movements she made or didn't make, that it didn't register really.

DAN: That's a good concept. What they're ready for next.

LAURA: So I thought that working with the dream and the dream content was more useful at this point, and I came to the body at the end.

JAN (to Dan): I had a thought, partly so much it's for me and I want to say it to you too, just the little bit that I did, plus the other things that are going on, the irony I'm feeling and that I saw with you is the irony that the things we think support us and sustain us and make us feel safe are the things that destroy us. And I see you taking those notes and her trying all day to get you to stop and you're filling up more pages and I was thinking about what I've done with my back that I thought was supporting my life and supporting me and it's really what, over time, destroyed it.

DAN: I want to say that I commend you on coming forward as you did, especially that you seemed critical earlier, and for you to come forward and openly explore something like that, I commend you for it.

LAURA:(to another group member) What's going on with you?

LEN: I'm just really appreciating you, really enjoying it.

LAURA: That was difficult to see, most of the time. You sit there nearly all the time — and I can't help noticing it because I'm directly opposite you — with a kind of grim expression on your face, or no expression.

LEN: I was really enjoying it, just enjoying it, taking it in, and marveling at it. I walk away with a sense of being with somebody who really knows just what to do. It's kind of like an awe thing.

LAURA: I am so aware of the tension in your face which is occasionally relieved by laughing when something funny happens, somebody says something. Do *you* need glasses all the time?

LEN: Unfortunately.

LAURA: Get a little closer and take them off. Let me see your face. What do you see now?

LEN: Still a little blurry, but it's better.

LAURA: That can get better only if you relax. I recommend that you close your eyes and let them fall back. Close them softly. See — you let them twitch now — keep breathing. Let your mouth loose. It's so covered up with your beard I can hardly see it, but there's a lot of tension. When you open your eyes, open them softly and just let come in what comes in. Don't grab.

LEN: Sol's red shirt — and your smile.

LAURA: You can see quite well.

LEN: It's really *quite* well, 'cause things really are clearer. It's weird.

LAURA: Leave them off as much as possible — when you don't actually need them, of course. It's a kind of wall. When you wear them, it's a kind of wall; it makes for distance.

LEN: I have to admit, I couldn't see his face hardly at all before and it's clear now.

LAURA: Well, when your eyes are more relaxed you see better.

LEN: I've just really been enjoying you.

LAURA: For people who don't have much experience in Gestalt, or have their kind of experience in what I call "West Coast Gestalt," they don't appreciate the minimal work, and I find that it is more easily assimilated and therefore keeps better, while the great excitements, they are kind of taken in and you spout it around and then you get rid of it again.

LEN: Just from watching you work with other people, I got some insights into myself, in terms of some things that I need to let go of, and I think there's still tension there because they still have to be dealt with but I think I know what I have to do and I guess that feels better.

LAURA: And you talk in a *should* language: "I know what I have to do."

LEN: I want to do it, I really do. It's just not going to be very pleasant.

LAURA: You look very different now.

LEN: It's getting clearer.

HAL: Want to work on a crazy child dream that I have?

LAURA: Yes.

HAL: It's good to work with you again, Laura. I had a dream a night or two ago, not remembering as much of it now as I did. I'm walking in the street and I'm seeing the largest, fattest, thickest, tallest weeds I've ever seen in my life. The street is filled with them and they are all purple. People are running away and I'm walking in the direction in which they are running away from. I am coming right around the corner of a building. There's a part of a body and I can only see the lowest portion, like a leg, and I begin to look up and it's a purple monster. I haven't had a monster dream since I was a very little boy and I'm 56 years old and it was the tallest, biggest, fattest, ugliest monster I've ever seen and it was solid purple. I become very frightened. That's all I remember.

LAURA: Be the monster.

HAL: You want me to get up and be the monster? You mean act the monster? "YAHHHHHH! I can kill. I have the power to kill. I am a purple people eater and I will eat you up."

LAURA: How do you feel as the monster?

HAL: Scared. Very scared. I feel it in here, I'm feeling it right now, in my stomach. It's tight. It's my anger. I'm very frightened of it. It's very powerful.

LAURA: Who are you angry with?

HAL: Beginning when? In the here and now. In the here and now I want to bury my hands.

LAURA: Otherwise you might do what?

HAL: Choke, beat, kill. Angry with my wife, angry with my kids. Very angry. I'm thinking right now of the weeds growing in my back yard.

LAURA: Be the weeds.

HAL: "We're ugly. Ugly weeds. Fuck up your gorgeous garden. You spent so much money and so much time and so much effort making your beautiful garden and we fuck it up, because nobody wants to pull us out. Look how ugly your garden looks now. Your beautiful Shangri-la is ugly, full of ugly weeds." The house that I bought two years ago that I put up for sale, and I really had weeds growing there, because nobody takes care of it.

LAURA: What do you do?

HAL: Suffer a lot. I'm not going to go pull the fuckin' weeds. Selling the house. I don't have the time to take care of weeds. I don't want to any more. The house didn't do for me what I wanted it to do. I'm thinking of how upset many of the people are who come to me for help, come with a head full of weeds and we pull out the weeds and you've got bare earth and it feels like it's empty but you have to wait for the flowers to grow and that takes time.

LAURA: To whom are you saying it?

HAL: Because I left my wife, early part of the summer.

AURA: That's why you can't get angry with her?

HAL: Oh, I can get angry with her. It's my kids I can't get angry with.

LAURA: Right now, make a dialogue with your kids. Take your hands out of your pockets.

HAL: I'm so goddammed confused with you all. On the one hand you tell me you're not passing judgment; but what you're doing makes so much noise I can't hear what you say. I see what you do constantly. You do make judgments. I'm pissed off at you. I think I'm pissed off.

LAURA: Try to feel how you are saying that, how you are holding yourself.

HAL: I'm holding myself down. I'm keeping my fingers spread apart.

LAURA: Is anybody listening to you?

HAL: I'm whining. Who's gonna listen to somebody who whines?

LAURA: Pick yourself up.

HAL: Agh! I'm remembering when I used to get angry my mother would call me bulldog. "Bulldog, what are you angry about?" Fucking angry with you kids 'cause you're stupid, because you make a choice to choose to believe one side of the story because I keep my mouth shut, kept my mouth shut for many years. Big joke in our family, everybody sees the Hal who's angry in the back-yard but nobody sees the Hal who got shitted on in the kitchen and then was told, "What are you angry about?

Keep your mouth shut, you sound like a bulldog." I'm feeling like a miserable wretch.

LAURA: Can you argue with your mother? Argue back. You're the bulldog.

HAL: "YAGHHHHHHHHHH! Fuck off! I feel so fuckin' angry. I really could be a people eater, I'm so fucking angry at you all. You counter it with stuff I can't fight back with and say things to me like, 'You're angry a lot? And if you don't believe you, what part do you play?' Fuck you kids! I paid a fortune for your therapy and you give me back this kind of shit."

LAURA: What do you expect? (Laughter)

HAL: God, I'm angry! Feel so powerless almost to do anything about it.

LAURA: What did you expect from therapy for your children? That they should be nice and quiet?

HAL: No. They should have respected their father. (Laughter) I think I would have expected for them at least to come to me and say, "Dad, what's your side of the story? Dad, what happened through all these years?"

LAURA: You want them to be like you, understanding and quiet and interested. And again you want the confluence.

HAL: They're not like me. They have to be what they are.

LAURA: You know, there's something I learned from my first analyst when I was 23 or 24 years old. Aggressive people you have to meet with their own weapons. If they are nasty to you, or noisy...

HAL: Usually I can do that with most people, but I don't do it with my kids.

LAURA: What are you afraid of?

HAL: Scared they'll leave me. I'll lose my grandchildren.

LAURA: As long as they need you they won't leave you.

HAL: I know that's true, I know. I had the dream before this weekend and I did some of this work in a workshop that I went to Friday and Saturday before we came here and I know I have to face up to them. I know. I took off the bracelet my wife gave me for my fiftieth birthday and threw it on the floor, ended up putting it in my pocket. I know I have to face them with my anger. Even if it doesn't go anywhere, I'll feel better.

LAURA: If you don't express it at the time something occurs that makes you angry, you accumulate a lot of resentment, a lot of unfinished business, and you poison yourself.

HAL: That's true. I recognize I'm the purple people eater. That part of me I can see. I don't know what part of me are the weeds, purple weeds.

LAURA: Be a weed. How do you feel?

HAL: Stuck! Stuck in the ground. Can't move. OK. I get it. I thank you.

LAURA: OK. I think our time is pretty much up.

"A Workshop with Laura Perls" is a transcription of a workshop conducted at the 25th Annual Institute of the American Academy of Psychotherapists which met in 1980 in New York City.

15.

Commitment

After a lifetime of involvement and concern with Gestalt therapy and theory, after thousands of sessions and workshops with clients and trainees and dozens of interviews on the history of Gestalt therapy and my part in it — after having been married to Fritz Perls for 40 years, living and working with and without him, and after having survived most of my old friends and family and almost all the cofounders of the New York Institute for Gestalt Therapy — I am a somewhat tired and rather reluctant speaker. So I am not going to bore you (or myself!) with another historical or theoretical discourse. Instead, I am going to tell you a story, a story that has fascinated me and stayed with me since I first saw a Japanese film called "The Woman in the Dunes." I have seen it several times; it has never failed to move and enchant me anew.

This is the story:

A man on a beach, having all day long collected and classified bugs and beetles, has missed the last bus back to the city. Looking for a place to stay overnight, he wanders around on top of the cliff, until he sees a light deep down in the dunes. Rope ladders are hanging down from the cliff and he climbs down to the house, where he finds a drab-looking lonely woman who takes him in for the night.

When he gets up in the morning, he discovers that the ladders have been pulled up by the village people, who are dancing and jeering on top of the cliff, and he realizes that he has been trapped. His futile attempts to find a way out leave him angry and desperate. But gradually he becomes aware of what is available and what may be possible within this confined situation. His growing attachment to the woman result in her becoming pregnant, and his need for activity and his scientific curiosity results in the invention of a device to trap water from the nightly fog and dew. When the time comes for the woman to give birth, the villagers let down the ladders and carry her up to the midwife. They leave the ladders hanging, and our scientist, if he wanted to, could now get out. But he chooses to stay.

Now why am I telling you this story, and what is it all about? It is a parable about *commitment*. When you are really committed, it is for better or for worse, for whatever may occur within the confinement of a situation; not only in marriage and family, but any relationship in which you have assumed responsibility, a profession, an art, a vocation, there is no way out. As long as our man in the story cannot accept the limitations of the situation, he feels trapped. When he accepts his confinement, possibilities within its boundaries become realities: the desert becomes fertile, the woman a mother. This opens the trap, the boundaries widen. By committing himself anew to the somewhat changed but still limited and difficult situation, the man takes responsibility for the *consequences* of his own creative activities. He himself has opened the trap of his own personal limitations, the conditioned habits, attitudes and prejudices, the fixed gestalten of his former life. By accepting and coping with "what is," he transforms and transcends the situation and achieves true freedom.

In my own life, I had many experiences when I felt trapped and resentful and desperately looked for a way out: going on strike or changing subjects during my student days, getting married and having a child instead of finishing my dissertation and getting my doctorate. But then I went back to Frankfurt and finished, in 1932, just a few months before we had to leave Germany. (After 50 years, the Psychology Department has renewed my diploma.)

In South Africa, I felt trapped by the tight provincial atmosphere, the diminutive number of congenial people, the tense and threatening political situation. But with no way out, I gradually came to realize that even if I had to stay within my one single room, I had walls of books, a grand piano and the whole classical piano literature, that even three lifetimes would not be enough to work through it all. This profoundly changed my life. In my practice I started to use face-to-face dialogue and body awareness; I wrote stories and poems. And Fritz and I started working on what became *Ego, Hunger and Aggression.* It was just the social and professional isolation and confinement that forced us to focus our interest on our own resources and mobilized our own creative potential, which had been mostly dormant within the limitations of psychoanalysis.

When I started to write poetry, I expected that it would be much easier to write free verse than strict stanzas or sonnets or any other traditionally regulated prosodic variation. But I found that just the opposite is true: without a developed sense of meter, rhyme and rhythm, free verse often becomes verbose and flabby, not much more than cut-up prose. By accepting the constraints of traditional prosody, unfathomed thoughts, ideas, insights and feelings emerge, come into focus, get condensed into memorable forms and images — complete gestalten.

One last example: After the publication of *Gestalt Therapy: Excitement and Growth in the Human Personality,* Fritz Perls and Paul Goodman were keen on starting an Institute for Gestalt Therapy. I did not want to be included, in spite of having been in most of the time on their discussions during the writing of the book. But when forty people turned up for Fritz's introductory lectures and workshop, he took twenty and I took twenty — and I felt trapped, resentful and afraid. I had never before worked with large groups, never taught any class, never spoken in public. I felt entirely unprepared and imposed upon. I floundered around, I got sick, I tried to coordinate my workshop with Fritz's lectures which did not work for me at all. By trial and error, I gradually developed my own approach, had my own trainees and groups, and continued working in New York. After thirty-five years I am still there, but the boundaries have widened — the ladders are down, and I am climbing in and out (lately with a little mechanical difficulty!).

Commitment is easiest when the limitations are imposed by the actual circumstances. You are literally *being* committed, first to the family, then to school, to study, to work, to a hospital, to prison, to a concentration camp. If you can't or won't take a way out, the commitment to what is possible within the confinement is lifesaving and life enhancing, even until death.

Commitment is much more difficult and for many people quite impossible, when there are choices. I found that particularly so with my most highly gifted, multitalented clients (in my own case, too) — the "Wunderkinder" to whom everything comes so easily that they don't learn to take time to seriously work through real difficulties. *Embarrass de richesse* (encumbered by riches), they drift noncommittally from one possibility to another, being promising in their early years and disappointing and disappointed in the long run.

Commitment requires discipline, and discipline implies limitations. In Gestalt therapy we impose limits through the actual structure of the therapeutic situation: the emphasis on present experience; by discouraging and interrupting deflections and other dummy activities; by exaggerating the self-inhibiting habits, principles, attitudes, muscular contractions and malcoordinations, bringing them into the foreground as still present activities, all *within* the safe − e.g., limited − therapeutic situation. Only when, through the de-automization of the fixed behavior gestalten, more support functions have become available, the truly creative adjustment becomes possible. The committed therapist has to know, but also must be able to control the expression of, his own impatience, his own ambition and competitiveness, his own anxiety.

Voluntary commitment demands sacrifices, the giving up of interests and involvements of value for the dedication to a greater value. This is the most difficult aspect of commitment. As the ladders are down, there are choices. The temptations are all around, even in the desert of one's own chosen dedication. There are periodically doubts and regrets, as I have experienced in my own life. But looking around here today at several generations of clients and students and co-workers and friends, I see the desert in bloom and I feel richly rewarded.

"Commitment" was delivered as the opening talk at *The Gestalt Journal*'s annual conference which met in Provincetown, Massachusetts, in 1985. It was published in Volume IX, Number 1, (spring, 1986) of *The Gestalt Journal.*